DEDICATION

PREFACE

INTRODUCTION

PART I: RETHINKING EDUCATION AND SKILLS

CHAPTER 1: REIMAGINING EDUCATION FOR THE AI AGE

CHAPTER 2: IN-DEMAND SKILLS AND CERTIFICATIONS

CHAPTER 3: LIFELONG LEARNING AND CONTINUOUS DEVELOPMENT

PART II: ADAPTING TO THE CHANGING WORKFORCE

CHAPTER 4: THE FLEXIBLE WORKFORCE

CHAPTER 5: EMBRACING TECHNOLOGICAL DISRUPTION

CHAPTER 6: COLLABORATION AND SOFT SKILLS

PART III: LEADERSHIP AND ORGANIZATIONAL STRATEGIES

CHAPTER 7: CULTIVATING AI-SAVVY LEADERS

CHAPTER 8: BUILDING AN AI-READY WORKFORCE

CHAPTER 9: DYNAMIC JOB CREATION AND ENTREPRENEURSHIP

CONCLUSION

Thank you for picking up my book. Your support means a lot, and I hope you find the read both enjoyable and insightful. Beyond being an author, my work extends into research and consultancy within organizational behavior and leadership. I engage with a broad spectrum of clients, from individuals to larger teams and organizations, offering guidance in leadership development.

For a deeper dive into my professional background and consulting philosophy, several websites are available. There, you'll also find my contact details. I'm eager to hear your thoughts on the book or discuss potential collaboration in leadership coaching.

Discover more about my work and other publications related to leadership and organizational behavior at my personal website, https://thomaspatrickhuber.com.

Learn about my specific approach to leadership coaching and consulting at https://elevateus.ch, the official website of my company.

Lastly, in case you want to reach out to me directly please send me an email at thomaspatrick@mac.com.

I appreciate your support in purchasing this book and look forward to connecting with you.

Wishing you an enlightening journey,

Thomas P Huber, PhD, MS ECS

Dedication

To all those shifting and changing their jobs, navigating the uncertainties of a rapidly evolving workforce.

To those worried about what the future holds, seeking guidance and reassurance in these transformative times.

To those prepared, constantly learning and adapting, embracing new challenges with resilience and optimism.

And to everyone interested in the changing job market, curious about the opportunities and innovations that lie ahead.

This book is for you. May it inspire, inform, and empower you to thrive in the age of AI.

Preface

The world of work is undergoing a profound transformation, driven by the relentless advance of artificial intelligence and automation. Jobs that once seemed secure are evolving, new roles are emerging, and the skills needed to thrive are changing at an unprecedented pace. As we stand at the cusp of this new era, understanding and adapting to these changes is not just beneficial but essential for survival and success.

"Employability in the AI Era: Thriving in a Tech-Driven World" was born out of a recognition of these seismic shifts. The idea for this book emerged from countless conversations with professionals, educators, business leaders, and students—all grappling with the same fundamental questions: How do we prepare for a future that is increasingly uncertain? What skills will be valued in an AI-driven economy? How can we ensure that we are not left behind in this technological revolution?

This book aims to provide answers to these questions and more. It offers a comprehensive guide to understanding the impact of AI on the job market and provides practical strategies for individuals and organizations to adapt and thrive. By rethinking education and skills, embracing lifelong learning, and fostering a culture of innovation and adaptability, we can turn the challenges of this new era into opportunities.

Throughout this book, you will find insights from experts in various fields, real-world examples of successful adaptation, and actionable advice designed to help you navigate your career in the age of AI. Whether you are a professional looking to upskill, a leader seeking to guide your organization through change, or simply someone interested in the future of work, this book is for you.

I dedicate this book to all those who are shifting and changing their jobs, to those who are worried about the future, to those who are prepared and eager to learn, and to everyone interested in the evolving job market. Your resilience, curiosity, and determination are the driving forces that will shape the future of work.

As you read through these pages, I hope you find not only valuable knowledge but also inspiration and encouragement. The AI era is not something to fear but a new frontier to explore, filled with possibilities for those willing to adapt and grow.

Welcome to the journey of thriving in a tech-driven world.

Sincerely,

Thomas P Huber PhD MS ECS

Introduction

The rapid advancement of artificial intelligence is transforming the job market and the workforce in ways we could have only imagined a few decades ago. From automating routine tasks to enhancing decision-making processes, AI is reshaping industries, creating new opportunities, and rendering some traditional roles obsolete. This transformative impact calls for a fundamental shift in how we approach our careers and skill development.

Adaptability and continuous learning have become crucial in this dynamic environment. No longer can we rely solely on the education and skills acquired at the start of our careers; we must embrace a mindset of lifelong learning and be prepared to continuously update our knowledge and abilities to stay relevant.

In this book, we will explore the key themes and structure necessary to navigate this new landscape effectively. We will delve into the importance of proactive career planning, understanding that employability now involves more than just possessing a set of skills—it requires the ability to anticipate and adapt to change.

The evolving definition of employability includes not only technical proficiency but also the capacity for critical thinking, creativity, and emotional intelligence. As we journey through this book, we will examine these themes in detail, offering insights and strategies to help you thrive in the age of AI.

Welcome to the exploration of the future of work, where adaptability, continuous learning, and proactive planning are your keys to success.

Artificial intelligence (AI) is rapidly altering the landscape of the job market and workforce, ushering in a new era of unprecedented change and transformation. As AI technologies continue to advance, their impact on various sectors and industries becomes increasingly profound, reshaping the nature of work and the skills required to succeed.

One of the most immediate and visible impacts of AI is automation. Routine, repetitive tasks across various industries are being increasingly automated, leading to significant changes in job roles. Manufacturing, logistics, customer service, and even some aspects of healthcare are seeing AI-driven systems and robots taking over tasks previously performed by humans. This automation can lead to job displacement, as roles that were once labor-intensive are now managed by machines.

While automation poses a threat to certain jobs, it also creates new opportunities. The rise of AI has given birth to entirely new job categories and roles that did not exist a decade ago. Fields such as data science, machine learning engineering, AI ethics, and AI operations are burgeoning, requiring specialized skills and knowledge. These new roles offer exciting career opportunities for those who are prepared to acquire the necessary expertise.

AI is not only about replacing human labor; it is also about augmenting human capabilities. AI tools and systems can assist workers in making better decisions, enhancing productivity, and performing complex tasks more efficiently. For example, in fields like healthcare, AI can analyze medical data to provide insights that aid doctors in diagnosis and treatment planning, leading to better patient outcomes.

As AI continues to permeate various industries, the skills required for many jobs are evolving. There is a growing demand for proficiency in digital literacy, coding, data analysis, and AI-related technologies. Moreover, skills such as critical thinking, creativity, and problem-solving are becoming increasingly valuable as they complement the capabilities of AI systems. Workers must be prepared to continually update their skill sets to remain competitive in the job market.

The integration of AI into the workplace is also shifting workforce dynamics. The traditional model of long-term, full-time employment is being supplemented by more flexible work arrangements. Remote work, gig economy jobs, and freelance opportunities are becoming more prevalent, driven by AI-powered platforms that connect workers with employers globally. This shift offers greater flexibility and work-life balance but also requires workers to be adaptable and self-motivated.

The widespread adoption of AI has significant economic and social implications. On one hand, it can drive economic growth by increasing productivity and efficiency. On the other hand, it may exacerbate income inequality and lead to job polarization, where high-skill and low-skill jobs grow, but middle-skill jobs decline. Policymakers and business leaders must address these challenges to ensure a fair and inclusive transition to an AI-driven economy.

The deployment of AI in the workplace raises important ethical considerations. Issues such as data privacy, algorithmic bias, and the transparency of AI decision-making processes need to be carefully managed. Companies must adopt ethical guidelines and practices to ensure that AI is used responsibly and that its benefits are shared broadly across society. The impact of AI on the job market and workforce underscores the need for proactive career planning and continuous learning. Individuals must embrace a lifelong learning mindset, staying informed about technological advancements and regularly updating their skills. Educational institutions and training programs must evolve to equip learners with the knowledge and abilities required in an AI-driven world.

The rapidly changing landscape of the modern job market, driven by advancements in artificial intelligence (AI) and technology, underscores the critical need for adaptability and continuous learning. As AI automates routine tasks and creates new job roles, individuals must be prepared to shift and evolve alongside these changes. This requires a mindset that embraces flexibility, openness to new experiences, and the willingness to acquire new skills throughout one's career.

Adaptability is now a key attribute for career success. The ability to pivot and adjust to new circumstances, whether it's learning how to use new technology, transitioning to a different role, or even switching industries, is invaluable. Those who can quickly adapt are better positioned to take advantage of new opportunities that arise from technological advancements. This flexibility also helps in mitigating the risks associated with job displacement, as adaptable workers can more easily move into new positions or fields.

Continuous learning is equally essential in this environment. The rapid pace of technological change means that the skills that are in demand today might not be the same tomorrow. Therefore, committing to lifelong learning is crucial. This involves not just formal education, but also informal learning through online courses, workshops, reading, and hands-on experience. By continuously updating their skills and knowledge, individuals can stay relevant and competitive in the job market.

Lifelong learning also fosters a growth mindset, which is the belief that abilities and intelligence can be developed with effort and time. This mindset encourages resilience and persistence, enabling individuals to overcome challenges and setbacks more effectively. It also promotes curiosity and innovation, as lifelong learners are often more open to exploring new ideas and experimenting with different approaches.

Organizations also play a significant role in promoting adaptability and continuous learning. By providing employees with access to training programs, learning resources, and opportunities for professional development, companies can cultivate a more skilled and versatile workforce. This not only enhances productivity and innovation but also helps in attracting and retaining top talent.

"Employability in the AI Era: Thriving in a Tech-Driven World" is structured to provide a comprehensive guide to navigating the evolving job market influenced by artificial intelligence. The book is divided into three main parts, each addressing critical aspects of adapting to and thriving in an AI-driven world.

The first part, "Rethinking Education and Skills," explores how traditional education models need to evolve to meet the demands of the AI age. It highlights the limitations of current educational systems and emphasizes the integration of AI and technology into curricula to foster critical thinking, creativity, and problem-solving skills. This section also delves into identifying high-demand skills in the AI era, the role of certifications and micro-credentials, and the importance of upskilling and reskilling programs. Moreover, it underscores the necessity of lifelong learning and provides strategies for effective self-directed learning, leveraging online resources and educational platforms, and building a personal learning network.

The second part, "Adapting to the Changing Workforce," focuses on the significant shifts in workforce dynamics due to AI. It discusses the rise of remote work and flexible work arrangements, the growth of the gig economy and freelancing opportunities, and the tools and technologies enabling these changes. This section examines how AI impacts various industries, identifies emerging job roles and new career paths, and stresses the importance of cultivating a growth mindset and adaptability. Additionally, it emphasizes the value of human-AI collaboration, enhancing communication and interpersonal skills, developing emotional intelligence and empathy, and fostering teamwork in an AI-augmented workplace.

The third part, "Leadership and Organizational Strategies," addresses how organizations and leaders can navigate the AI transformation. It explores the roles of leaders in guiding AI integration, developing AI literacy and strategic thinking, and leading with empathy and ethical considerations. This section provides insights into promoting a culture of innovation and continuous learning within organizations, strategies for talent acquisition and retention, and investing in employee development and reskilling initiatives. Furthermore, it discusses identifying opportunities in the AI economy, supporting entrepreneurship and innovation, and the role of public-private partnerships and policy implications for a dynamic job market.

Throughout the book, key themes are interwoven to provide a cohesive understanding of how to thrive in the AI era. These themes include the critical need for adaptability and continuous learning, the importance of proactive career planning, and the evolving definition of employability that goes beyond technical skills to include critical thinking, creativity, and emotional intelligence. The book emphasizes the significance of a growth mindset, the integration of technology into education and work, and the development of a culture that values innovation and lifelong learning.

By combining expert insights, practical strategies, and real-world examples, "Employability in the AI Era" aims to empower individuals and organizations to proactively shape their futures. It offers a roadmap for professionals seeking to upskill, leaders aiming to future-proof their organizations, and entrepreneurs exploring new ventures. The book underscores the importance of embracing change, fostering human-AI collaboration, and building a resilient and dynamic workforce ready to face the challenges and opportunities of the AI age.

Proactive career planning has become increasingly important in the dynamic landscape of the modern workforce, particularly in the era of artificial intelligence and rapid technological advancements. The pace at which industries are evolving demands that individuals take a forward-thinking approach to their careers, ensuring they are not only prepared for current opportunities but also equipped to navigate future changes and challenges.

One of the primary reasons proactive career planning is essential is the unpredictability of the job market. AI and automation are transforming job roles at an unprecedented rate, making it difficult to predict which skills will be in demand in the coming years. By engaging in proactive career planning, individuals can anticipate these changes and strategically position themselves to take advantage of emerging opportunities. This involves regularly assessing industry trends, identifying potential growth areas, and acquiring new skills that align with future demands.

This kind of career planning fosters a mindset of continuous learning and adaptability. In an environment where technological advancements can quickly render certain skills obsolete, the ability to learn and adapt becomes a critical asset. Individuals who plan their careers proactively are more likely to invest in lifelong learning, seek out new educational opportunities, and stay updated on the latest developments in their field. This commitment to continuous improvement not only enhances their employability but also allows them to remain competitive and relevant in a rapidly changing job market.

Another significant aspect of proactive career planning is the empowerment it provides. When individuals take charge of their career trajectory, they are better able to set clear goals, identify their strengths and weaknesses, and create a roadmap for achieving their professional aspirations. This sense of direction and purpose can lead to greater job satisfaction and fulfillment, as individuals are actively working towards their desired outcomes rather than passively reacting to external circumstances. Additionally, proactive planning can help individuals build a robust professional network, seek out mentorship opportunities, and gain valuable experiences that contribute to their long-term success.

Careers guided by proactivity also mitigates the risks associated with job displacement. As AI and automation continue to reshape the workforce, certain job roles may become redundant or significantly altered. Individuals who have a proactive career plan are better prepared to pivot when necessary, transitioning into new roles or industries with greater ease. This ability to adapt and find alternative career paths reduces the anxiety and uncertainty that often accompany job displacement, providing a sense of security and resilience.

Organizations benefit from employees who engage in proactive career planning. These individuals are typically more motivated, forward-thinking, and invested in their professional development, which can lead to higher productivity and innovation within the workplace. Companies that support and encourage proactive career planning through training programs, development opportunities, and career coaching are more likely to attract and retain top talent. This not only enhances the organization's competitive edge but also fosters a culture of continuous improvement and adaptability, which is crucial in an AI-driven world.

In the broader context, proactive career planning contributes to a more dynamic and resilient economy. When individuals are equipped to navigate career transitions and seize new opportunities, the workforce as a whole becomes more agile and capable of responding to economic shifts. This adaptability is essential for sustaining economic growth and stability in the face of technological disruptions.

The definition of employability is undergoing a significant transformation in the age of artificial intelligence and rapid technological advancement. Traditionally, employability referred to the possession of specific skills, qualifications, and experiences that made an individual suitable for a particular job. However, as the job market evolves, so too does the concept of employability, expanding to encompass a broader range of attributes that reflect the complexities and demands of a modern workforce.

In today's dynamic environment, employability is no longer limited to technical expertise and formal education. While these factors remain important, they are now seen as just one piece of a much larger puzzle. The evolving definition of employability includes a combination of hard skills, soft skills, and personal attributes that enable individuals to thrive in various roles and adapt to changing circumstances.

One of the most significant shifts in this new definition is the emphasis on lifelong learning. The rapid pace of technological change means that the skills required for many jobs are constantly evolving. Therefore, being employable now means being committed to continuous learning and development. This involves not only staying current with industry trends and advancements but also being proactive in acquiring new skills and knowledge.

Lifelong learners are more adaptable and better prepared to meet the challenges of a changing job market, making them highly valuable to employers.

Adaptability itself has become a crucial component of employability. The ability to pivot in response to new technologies, market demands, and organizational changes is essential. Employers are increasingly looking for individuals who can demonstrate flexibility and resilience, who are not only able to cope with change but can also drive and manage it. This adaptability extends beyond technical skills to include the capacity for creative problem-solving and the ability to navigate complex and ambiguous situations. Another key element of the evolving definition of employability is emotional intelligence. As AI and automation take over routine and data-driven tasks, the human aspects of work become more important. Emotional intelligence encompasses the ability to understand and manage one's own emotions, as well as the ability to empathize with others, build strong interpersonal relationships, and navigate social complexities. High emotional intelligence is linked to better teamwork, leadership, and communication skills, all of which are increasingly valued in the modern workplace.

Employability today also includes a strong emphasis on critical thinking and problem-solving abilities. As machines handle more repetitive tasks, the demand for humans to engage in higher-order thinking and complex problem-solving grows. Employers seek individuals who can analyze information, think critically, and devise innovative solutions to problems. These skills are essential for driving progress and maintaining a competitive edge in a rapidly changing business landscape.

In addition to these attributes, the evolving definition of employability recognizes the importance of a proactive and entrepreneurial mindset. This involves taking initiative, being self-motivated, and possessing a sense of ownership over one's work and career development. An entrepreneurial mindset also includes the willingness to take risks, experiment with new ideas, and embrace failure as a learning opportunity. Individuals who exhibit these traits are often seen as more capable of contributing to organizational growth and innovation.

Cultural and global awareness have also become important factors in employability. As businesses operate in increasingly diverse and interconnected environments, the ability to work effectively across cultures and understand global market dynamics is crucial. This includes being open to different perspectives, demonstrating cultural sensitivity, and possessing the skills to collaborate with international teams. Furthermore, the integration of digital literacy into the concept of employability cannot be overlooked. In an era where digital tools and platforms are ubiquitous, having a strong foundation in digital literacy is essential. This includes not only technical proficiency with various software and tools but also an understanding of digital ethics, data privacy, and the implications of digital transformation on business practices.

The evolving definition of employability in the age of AI and technological advancement is multifaceted and dynamic. It encompasses a blend of technical skills, lifelong learning, adaptability, emotional intelligence, critical thinking, a proactive mindset, cultural awareness, and digital literacy. As the job market continues to evolve, individuals who embody these qualities will be better positioned to succeed and thrive. For employers, recognizing and cultivating these attributes in their workforce will be key to navigating the complexities of the modern business landscape and achieving long-term success.

Part I: Rethinking Education and Skills

In the era of artificial intelligence, the landscape of education and skills development is undergoing a radical transformation. Traditional models of education, which have long been the cornerstone of workforce preparation, are now being challenged by the rapid pace of technological advancements. This part of the book, "Rethinking Education and Skills," explores the necessity of overhauling our educational paradigms to better equip individuals for the demands of the AI age. As we delve into the intricacies of reimagining education, identifying in-demand skills, and fostering a culture of lifelong learning, it becomes clear that adaptability and continuous improvement are the keys to thriving in a constantly evolving job market.

The traditional education models, characterized by rigid curricula and standardized testing, are increasingly proving inadequate in preparing students for the complexities of the modern workforce. These models often emphasize rote memorization and the accumulation of static knowledge, neglecting the development of critical thinking, creativity, and problem-solving skills. As a result, graduates frequently find themselves ill-equipped to navigate the dynamic challenges posed by AI and other emerging technologies. The limitations of these conventional systems are becoming more apparent as the gap between educational outcomes and industry requirements widens. To bridge this gap, it is essential to rethink and redesign our educational approaches to foster the skills and mindsets necessary for success in the AI age.

Integrating AI and technology into curricula is a pivotal step towards modernizing education. This integration involves incorporating AI tools and applications into teaching methods, enabling students to gain firsthand experience with technologies that are reshaping the workforce. By using AI-driven educational platforms, educators can personalize learning experiences, catering to individual student needs and pacing. This approach not only enhances engagement and retention but also prepares students to work with and alongside AI systems. Furthermore, understanding AI's potential and limitations helps students develop a critical perspective on technology, enabling them to leverage it effectively in their future careers.

Fostering critical thinking and problem-solving skills is another crucial aspect of reimagining education for the AI age. Unlike traditional education, which often prioritizes the absorption of established knowledge, a modern curriculum should encourage students to question, analyze, and synthesize information. Critical thinking involves evaluating evidence, identifying biases, and making reasoned decisions, while problem-solving skills require creativity, persistence, and the ability to approach challenges from multiple angles. By embedding these skills into educational practices, we can equip students with the tools needed to navigate complex, real-world problems and adapt to unforeseen changes in their professional lives.

Encouraging creativity and innovation in education is essential for nurturing the next generation of thinkers and leaders. Creativity, often stifled by conventional educational methods, can be unleashed through project-based learning, interdisciplinary studies, and opportunities for experimentation. Innovation thrives in environments where students are allowed to explore ideas without the fear of failure, fostering a mindset that values curiosity and risk-taking. By promoting creativity, educational institutions can help students develop original solutions and approaches, driving progress in various fields and industries influenced by AI.

Collaborative learning and interdisciplinary approaches further enhance the educational experience, reflecting the interconnected nature of modern problems and industries. Collaborative learning encourages students to work together, share diverse perspectives, and develop interpersonal skills essential for teamwork in professional settings. Interdisciplinary education breaks down traditional subject barriers, integrating knowledge from various fields to provide a more holistic understanding of complex issues. This approach mirrors the multifaceted nature of challenges in the AI age, where solutions often require knowledge and skills from multiple domains. By fostering collaboration and interdisciplinary learning, we prepare students to tackle problems in innovative and comprehensive ways.

Identifying high-demand skills in the AI era is crucial for aligning education with workforce needs. As AI continues to transform industries, skills such as data analysis, machine learning, cybersecurity, and digital literacy are becoming increasingly valuable. Additionally, soft skills like critical thinking, communication, and emotional intelligence remain essential, as they complement technical abilities and enhance overall employability.

The role of certifications and micro-credentials in career advancement cannot be overstated. These credentials provide tangible proof of an individual's skills and knowledge, often in specific, high-demand areas. Unlike traditional degrees, certifications can be obtained relatively quickly and are frequently updated to reflect the latest industry standards and technologies. They offer a flexible and accessible way for individuals to upskill and stay competitive in the job market.

Popular upskilling and reskilling programs are becoming more prevalent as the need for continuous learning grows. These programs, often offered by educational institutions, online platforms, and employers, provide opportunities for workers to acquire new skills or transition into different roles. They are particularly valuable in helping individuals adapt to technological changes and shifting job demands.

Industry-specific skill requirements highlight the importance of tailored educational pathways. Different sectors have unique needs and challenges, necessitating specialized training and expertise. By aligning educational programs with industry requirements, we can ensure that graduates are well-prepared to meet the demands of their chosen fields.

The importance of technical and non-technical skills in the AI era underscores the need for a balanced skill set. While technical skills such as programming, data analysis, and AI literacy are crucial, non-technical skills like problem-solving, creativity, and collaboration are equally important. This combination of skills enables individuals to leverage technology effectively while also contributing to innovative and adaptive workplaces.

The necessity of being an active lifelong learner is a cornerstone of success in the AI era. As technologies evolve and job requirements change, the ability to continuously acquire new knowledge and skills becomes essential. Lifelong learning ensures that individuals remain adaptable, capable of meeting new challenges, and open to evolving career opportunities.

Effective self-directed learning strategies empower individuals to take charge of their own development. This involves setting clear goals, identifying resources, and regularly assessing progress. Self-directed learners are proactive in seeking out information, experimenting with new ideas, and applying what they learn in practical contexts.

Utilizing online resources and educational platforms is a powerful way to facilitate continuous learning. The internet offers a vast array of courses, tutorials, webinars, and other learning materials that can be accessed at any time. These resources make it easier for individuals to learn at their own pace, on their own schedule, and often at a lower cost than traditional education.

Balancing formal and informal learning opportunities is important for comprehensive development. Formal education provides structured learning and recognized credentials, while informal learning offers flexibility and the ability to explore interests and skills outside of traditional academic settings. Both forms of learning are valuable and should complement each other to create a well-rounded educational experience.

Building a personal learning network is an effective way to support lifelong learning. This network can include mentors, peers, industry professionals, and online communities that provide support, guidance, and resources. Engaging with a learning network helps individuals stay motivated, gain new perspectives, and access valuable information and opportunities for professional growth.

Chapter 1: Reimagining Education for the AI Age

The dawn of the AI era demands a radical transformation in our approach to education. Traditional education models, long considered the bedrock of learning and skill development, are increasingly proving inadequate in preparing individuals for the complexities and dynamism of the modern workforce. These models, characterized by rigid curricula, standardized testing, and a focus on rote memorization, often fail to equip students with the skills necessary to thrive in an AI-driven world. The limitations of these conventional systems are becoming more apparent as the gap between educational outcomes and industry requirements widens, necessitating a comprehensive rethinking of how we educate and prepare future generations.

Educators should integrate AI and technology into curricula which will be a pivotal step towards modernizing education and aligning it with the demands of the AI age. This integration involves more than just teaching students about AI; it requires the incorporation of AI tools and applications into everyday learning processes. By leveraging AI-driven educational platforms, educators can personalize learning experiences to cater to individual student needs and pacing, enhancing engagement and retention. These technologies enable students to gain firsthand experience with the tools that are reshaping industries, preparing them to work with and alongside AI systems in their future careers. Moreover, understanding the potential and limitations of AI helps students develop a critical perspective on technology, empowering them to use it responsibly and effectively.

We must foster critical thinking and problem-solving skills that are crucial in an educational landscape transformed by AI. Traditional education often prioritizes the accumulation of established knowledge, leaving little room for the development of analytical and evaluative abilities. However, the AI age demands that students are not just consumers of information, but active participants in its analysis and application. Critical thinking involves the ability to evaluate evidence, identify biases, and make reasoned decisions, while problem-solving skills require creativity, persistence, and the ability to approach challenges from multiple angles. By embedding these skills into educational practices, we can equip students with the tools needed to navigate complex, real-world problems and adapt to unforeseen changes in their professional lives.

Encouraging creativity and innovation in education is essential for nurturing the next generation of thinkers and leaders. Creativity, often stifled by conventional educational methods, can be unleashed through project-based learning, interdisciplinary studies, and opportunities for experimentation. Innovation thrives in environments where students are allowed to explore ideas without the fear of failure, fostering a mindset that values curiosity and risk-taking. By promoting creativity, educational institutions can help students develop original solutions and approaches, driving progress in various fields and industries influenced by AI.

Collaborative learning and interdisciplinary approaches further enhance the educational experience, reflecting the interconnected nature of modern problems and industries. Collaborative learning encourages students to work together, share diverse perspectives, and develop interpersonal skills essential for teamwork in professional settings. Interdisciplinary education breaks down traditional subject barriers, integrating knowledge from various fields to provide a more holistic understanding of complex issues. This approach mirrors the multifaceted nature of challenges in the AI age, where solutions often require knowledge and skills from multiple domains. By fostering collaboration and interdisciplinary learning, we prepare students to tackle problems in innovative and comprehensive ways.

The limitations of traditional education models are becoming increasingly evident in the face of rapid technological advancements and the evolving demands of the modern workforce. These conventional systems, characterized by rigid curricula, standardized testing, and a predominant focus on rote memorization, often fall short in preparing students for the complexities and dynamic nature of today's job market. Traditional education primarily emphasizes the acquisition of established knowledge, which, while important, does not sufficiently cultivate the critical thinking, creativity, and problem-solving skills that are essential in an AI-driven world.

One of the most significant limitations of traditional education models is their inflexibility. The standardized approach to teaching and assessment fails to account for the diverse learning styles and paces of individual students. This one-size-fits-all methodology often leads to disengagement and a lack of motivation among students who do not fit the mold. Moreover, the heavy reliance on standardized testing as the primary measure of student achievement tends to prioritize short-term memorization over long-term understanding and application of knowledge. This focus on testing can stifle creativity and discourage risk-taking, as students and teachers alike are pressured to "teach to the test" rather than explore innovative and interdisciplinary approaches to learning.

Another critical shortcoming is the disconnect between what is taught in traditional education settings and the skills needed in the modern workforce. The rapid pace of technological change means that the job market is constantly evolving, yet the curricula in many educational institutions remain static and outdated. Subjects that are crucial in today's world, such as digital literacy, data analysis, and AI, are often underrepresented or absent in traditional curricula. This gap leaves graduates ill-prepared for the demands of contemporary jobs, where proficiency in these areas is increasingly crucial. Additionally, traditional education systems often do not place enough emphasis on soft skills like communication, teamwork, and emotional intelligence, which are indispensable in the collaborative and interconnected nature of modern workplaces.

Traditional education models also tend to compartmentalize knowledge into distinct subjects, creating silos that can hinder interdisciplinary thinking and problem-solving. In the real world, complex problems do not fall neatly into categories; they require a multifaceted approach that draws on diverse fields of knowledge. The lack of integration across different subjects in traditional education systems means that students often miss out on opportunities to develop a holistic understanding of issues and to apply their learning in innovative ways. This siloed approach can limit students' ability to think critically and creatively about how to address real-world challenges Traditional education systems often lack the agility to respond to the rapidly changing landscape of skills and knowledge required by new technologies. Curricula updates can be slow and bureaucratic, meaning that by the time new content is introduced, it may already be outdated. This lag in adapting to current technological trends leaves students at a disadvantage, as they are not equipped with the most relevant and up-to-date skills needed in the workforce. Furthermore, the traditional teacher-centered model of education, where instructors are the primary source of knowledge, can limit opportunities for students to engage in self-directed learning and to develop the autonomy and initiative that are crucial for success in a rapidly changing world.

The emphasis on hierarchical, teacher-led instruction in traditional models can also impede the development of important life skills such as independent thinking, decision-making, and self-management. In a world where continuous learning and adaptability are key, students need to be equipped with the ability to learn independently, seek out new information, and adapt to new circumstances. Traditional education often does not provide sufficient opportunities for students to take ownership of their learning journey, explore their interests, and develop the self-directed learning habits that are essential for lifelong learning.

Integrating AI and technology into curricula represents a profound shift in educational practices, aligning learning environments with the demands of a rapidly evolving digital world. The incorporation of AI into educational settings goes beyond merely teaching students about artificial intelligence; it involves embedding AI-driven tools and technologies into the fabric of the learning process itself. This integration can significantly enhance the personalization, engagement, and effectiveness of education, preparing students not just to participate in, but to lead, an increasingly technology-driven society.

One of the key benefits of integrating AI into curricula is the ability to personalize learning experiences. AI-driven educational platforms can analyze individual student data to tailor instruction to each learner's unique needs, strengths, and areas for improvement. This level of customization allows for differentiated instruction that can accommodate various learning styles and paces, ensuring that no student is left behind. For instance, AI can provide real-time feedback and adaptive learning paths, enabling students to progress at their own speed and receive targeted support where needed. This personalized approach not only improves academic outcomes but also enhances student engagement and motivation by making learning more relevant and accessible.

AI and technology can significantly enrich the educational content and resources available to students. Through AI-powered tools, students can access a wealth of interactive and multimedia materials that make complex concepts more understandable and engaging. Virtual reality (VR) and augmented reality (AR) technologies, for example, can bring abstract theories to life, providing immersive learning experiences that traditional textbooks cannot match. AI can also facilitate advanced simulations and modeling in subjects such as science and engineering, allowing students to experiment and explore in ways that were previously impossible. These technologies help to deepen understanding and foster a more profound interest in the subject matter.

The integration of AI into curricula also prepares students for the future workforce by equipping them with essential digital literacy skills. As AI becomes ubiquitous in various industries, having a foundational understanding of AI principles and technologies becomes crucial. By incorporating AI into the curriculum, educational institutions can ensure that students are not only familiar with these technologies but also capable of using them effectively. This includes understanding how AI algorithms work, the ethical considerations surrounding AI, and the potential impacts of AI on society. Such knowledge is vital for future professionals who will need to navigate an AI-driven world, making informed decisions and contributing to the responsible development and deployment of AI technologies.

AI can enhance the efficiency and effectiveness of educational administration. AI-driven systems can streamline administrative tasks such as grading, scheduling, and resource allocation, freeing up valuable time for educators to focus on teaching and student support. These systems can also provide valuable insights into student performance and engagement, enabling data-driven decision-making that can improve educational outcomes. For example, predictive analytics can identify students at risk of falling behind, allowing for timely interventions and support. This proactive approach can help to improve retention rates and ensure that all students have the opportunity to succeed.

Technology and AI integration into curricula also encourages collaborative learning and fosters a sense of global connectivity. AI-powered platforms can facilitate communication and collaboration among students, both within and beyond the classroom. Students can work together on projects, share insights, and learn from one another, regardless of their physical location. This connectivity is particularly valuable in a globalized world, where the ability to collaborate across cultures and geographies is increasingly important. AI can support language translation, cultural exchange, and international collaboration, broadening students' perspectives and preparing them for a globalized workforce.

The integration of AI into education can drive innovation in teaching practices. Educators can use AI tools to design more engaging and effective lesson plans, incorporate real-time data into their teaching, and experiment with new instructional strategies. AI can provide insights into what works best for different types of learners, enabling continuous improvement and innovation in teaching. By leveraging AI, educators can become facilitators of learning rather than mere transmitters of knowledge, creating dynamic and interactive learning environments that inspire and motivate students.

Fostering critical thinking and problem-solving skills is an essential goal for modern education, especially in an era dominated by rapid technological advancements and an ever-evolving job market. These skills are paramount for preparing students to navigate complex, real-world challenges and to succeed in diverse professional environments. Traditional education models often emphasize memorization and the regurgitation of information, which, while important, do not adequately equip students with the ability to think independently, analyze situations critically, and devise innovative solutions to problems.

Critical thinking is the ability to objectively analyze and evaluate an issue in order to form a judgment. It involves a disciplined process of actively conceptualizing, applying, analyzing, synthesizing, and evaluating information gathered from observation, experience, reflection, reasoning, or communication. In fostering critical thinking, educators must encourage students to question assumptions, consider multiple perspectives, and reflect on the validity of their own beliefs and those of others. This process helps students to develop a deeper understanding of subjects and to apply their knowledge in practical, meaningful ways. Teaching methods such as Socratic questioning, debate, and case studies are particularly effective in promoting critical thinking. These approaches challenge students to think deeply, articulate their reasoning, and engage in rigorous intellectual discourse.

Problem-solving skills, on the other hand, involve the ability to identify complex problems, develop feasible solutions, and implement them effectively. Problem-solving is inherently tied to critical thinking, as it requires the ability to analyze situations, synthesize information, and evaluate possible outcomes. To cultivate these skills, educators must create learning environments that encourage experimentation, resilience, and creative thinking. Project-based learning is an excellent strategy for developing problem-solving abilities. By engaging in projects that address real-world issues, students learn to apply their theoretical knowledge, work collaboratively, and persist through challenges to find effective solutions. This hands-on approach not only enhances their problem-solving skills but also builds their confidence and resilience.

Integrating interdisciplinary learning is another powerful way to foster critical thinking and problem-solving. Real-world problems are rarely confined to a single discipline; they often require knowledge and skills from multiple fields. By breaking down the traditional silos of subject areas, interdisciplinary education encourages students to draw connections between different domains of knowledge, promoting a more holistic and nuanced understanding of complex issues. For example, a project that combines elements of science, technology, engineering, and mathematics (STEM) with humanities and social sciences can provide a richer context for problem-solving and critical thinking. This approach helps students to see the broader implications of their work and to appreciate the interconnectedness of various disciplines.

Encouraging a growth mindset is also crucial for fostering these skills. A growth mindset, as opposed to a fixed mindset, is the belief that abilities and intelligence can be developed through dedication and hard work. This mindset fosters a love of learning and a resilience that is essential for great accomplishment. When students believe that their intelligence and skills can improve with effort, they are more likely to take on challenges, persevere through difficulties, and view failures as opportunities for growth. Educators can cultivate a growth mindset by praising effort rather than innate ability, encouraging perseverance, and providing constructive feedback that focuses on the learning process.

The use of technology and digital tools can further enhance the development of critical thinking and problem-solving skills. AI-powered educational platforms can offer personalized learning experiences that adapt to the needs and abilities of individual students, providing targeted challenges that stimulate critical thinking. Interactive simulations and virtual labs allow students to experiment with variables, test hypotheses, and observe outcomes in a risk-free environment, fostering a deeper understanding of scientific and mathematical principles. Moreover, collaborative tools enable students to work together on problem-solving tasks, sharing ideas and resources in real-time, regardless of their physical location. This not only enhances their problem-solving abilities but also prepares them for the collaborative nature of modern work environments.

Fostering these skills requires a shift in assessment practices. Traditional assessments, which often emphasize the recall of information, do not adequately measure students' critical thinking and problem-solving abilities. Alternative assessment methods, such as portfolios, performance tasks, and reflective journals, can provide a more accurate and comprehensive evaluation of these skills. These assessments allow students to demonstrate their thought processes, creativity, and problem-solving strategies, providing valuable insights into their learning and development Encouraging creativity and innovation in education is vital for preparing students to thrive in an increasingly complex and dynamic world. The traditional education system, with its rigid curricula and emphasis on standardized testing, often stifles the creative potential of students. To foster a generation of innovators and creative thinkers, it is essential to create an educational environment that nurtures curiosity, experimentation, and the willingness to take risks.

Creativity in education involves more than just artistic expression; it encompasses the ability to think outside the box, to approach problems from novel perspectives, and to develop original solutions. Innovation, on the other hand, is the application of creative ideas to generate value, whether through new products, processes, or methodologies. Encouraging these traits in students requires a shift away from rote learning and towards a more holistic, student-centered approach to education.

One effective way to encourage creativity and innovation is through project-based learning (PBL). PBL allows students to work on projects that are meaningful and relevant to their lives, thereby increasing engagement and motivation. These projects often address real-world problems, requiring students to apply their knowledge in practical, often interdisciplinary ways. By working on extended projects, students have the opportunity to explore their interests deeply, to collaborate with peers, and to develop a range of skills, from research and critical thinking to communication and teamwork. This approach not only fosters creativity but also helps students see the relevance of their education to the world beyond the classroom.

Another powerful strategy is to integrate opportunities for creative expression and experimentation across all subjects. This can be achieved by incorporating activities that encourage divergent thinking, such as brainstorming sessions, mind mapping, and design thinking exercises. In science and mathematics, for example, students can be challenged to develop multiple solutions to a problem or to design experiments that test unconventional hypotheses. In language arts, creative writing assignments can encourage students to explore different genres and styles, while in social studies, role-playing and simulations can help them understand complex historical events and social dynamics from multiple perspectives.

Teachers play a crucial role in fostering creativity and innovation. They must create a classroom environment that is open, supportive, and conducive to risk-taking. This means encouraging students to ask questions, to express their ideas freely, and to view failures as learning opportunities rather than setbacks. Teachers can model creative thinking by demonstrating their own problem-solving processes, sharing their own creative projects, and celebrating creative efforts in the classroom. Professional development for teachers should include training on how to nurture creativity and innovation, equipping them with the tools and strategies to inspire their students.

The physical and digital learning environments also significantly impact creativity and innovation. Classrooms should be flexible spaces that can be easily reconfigured for different activities, such as group work, independent study, and presentations. Access to a variety of materials and resources, from art supplies to technology tools, allows students to experiment and create in different ways. Digital platforms can facilitate collaboration and creativity by providing tools for virtual brainstorming, digital storytelling, and multimedia presentations. Makerspaces, equipped with tools like 3D printers, robotics kits, and software for coding and design, provide students with hands-on opportunities to bring their ideas to life.

Assessment methods must also evolve to support creativity and innovation. Traditional tests and quizzes, which primarily measure rote memorization, are inadequate for evaluating creative thinking and innovative problem-solving. Alternative assessment methods, such as portfolios, performance tasks, and peer reviews, allow students to demonstrate their creative processes and outcomes. These assessments can capture a broader range of student skills and achievements, providing a more comprehensive picture of their abilities. Feedback should be constructive and focused on the creative process, encouraging students to reflect on their work, to iterate on their ideas, and to continue developing their creative skills.

Partnerships with external organizations, such as businesses, cultural institutions, and community groups, can provide valuable opportunities for students to engage in creative and innovative projects. These partnerships can bring real-world relevance to classroom activities, offering students insights into how creativity and innovation are applied in various fields. Internships, mentorship programs, and collaborative projects with professionals can expose students to different career paths and inspire them to pursue their own creative endeavors.

Encouraging creativity and innovation in education also involves fostering a culture of curiosity and lifelong learning. Students should be encouraged to pursue their passions and interests, both within and outside of the classroom. This might involve supporting extracurricular activities, such as clubs and competitions, that allow students to explore new areas and to develop their creative talents. Encouraging reading, exploration, and the use of digital tools for self-directed learning can help students cultivate a mindset of continuous growth and innovation.

Collaborative learning and interdisciplinary approaches represent pivotal shifts in educational strategies, reflecting the interconnected nature of modern knowledge and the collaborative demands of today's workforce. These methods break away from traditional, isolated modes of learning, fostering environments where students can engage with diverse perspectives, work together towards common goals, and apply knowledge across various disciplines to solve complex problems. Embracing these approaches can significantly enhance educational outcomes, preparing students for the multifaceted challenges they will encounter in their professional lives. This kind of learning involves students working together in groups to explore concepts, complete tasks, and achieve shared learning objectives. This approach encourages the exchange of ideas, critical discussion, and mutual support, helping students develop essential interpersonal skills such as communication, teamwork, and conflict resolution.

When students collaborate, they learn to appreciate different viewpoints, build on each other's strengths, and negotiate solutions, all of which are crucial skills in both academic and professional settings. Collaborative learning also promotes deeper understanding as students explain concepts to one another, ask questions, and engage in peer teaching, which reinforces their own knowledge and comprehension.

Interdisciplinary approaches, on the other hand, integrate knowledge and methods from different disciplines to provide a more holistic understanding of complex issues. Traditional education often segments knowledge into discrete subjects, which can limit students' ability to see connections between different areas of study. By adopting interdisciplinary approaches, educators can help students develop a more comprehensive perspective that mirrors the interconnectedness of real-world problems. For example, addressing climate change effectively requires knowledge from environmental science, economics, political science, and social studies. Through interdisciplinary projects, students learn to synthesize information from multiple sources, think critically about how different fields intersect, and apply a broad range of skills and knowledge to develop innovative solutions.

The benefits of collaborative learning and interdisciplinary approaches extend beyond academic performance. These methods foster a sense of community and belonging among students, creating a supportive learning environment where everyone feels valued and included. This sense of belonging can enhance motivation and engagement, leading to higher levels of student satisfaction and retention.

Moreover, these approaches prepare students for the collaborative nature of modern workplaces, where teamwork and cross-disciplinary collaboration are often essential for success. By working together on interdisciplinary projects, students develop the skills and attitudes necessary to thrive in diverse, dynamic professional environments.

Implementing collaborative learning and interdisciplinary approaches requires thoughtful planning and a willingness to innovate. Teachers play a crucial role in facilitating these methods, acting as guides and mentors rather than mere transmitters of knowledge. Effective facilitation involves creating opportunities for meaningful interaction, providing guidance and support as needed, and fostering an inclusive environment where all students feel comfortable contributing. This might involve using techniques such as group discussions, peer reviews, collaborative projects, and problem-based learning scenarios. Teachers can also help students develop the skills needed for effective collaboration, such as active listening, constructive feedback, and conflict resolution.

The physical and digital learning environments must also support collaborative and interdisciplinary learning. Classrooms should be designed to facilitate group work, with flexible seating arrangements and access to a variety of resources. Digital tools and platforms can enhance collaboration by enabling students to communicate and share information in real-time, regardless of their physical location. Online discussion forums, collaborative documents, and project management tools can help students work together more efficiently and effectively. Furthermore, technology can support interdisciplinary learning by providing access to a wide range of resources and enabling students to conduct research and analysis across different fields.

Assessment methods must align with the goals of collaborative and interdisciplinary learning. Traditional tests and quizzes may not adequately capture the depth and breadth of understanding that these approaches foster. Alternative assessment methods, such as group projects, portfolios, presentations, and reflective essays, can provide a more comprehensive evaluation of students' abilities to collaborate, think critically, and apply interdisciplinary knowledge. These assessments can also encourage students to take ownership of their learning, reflect on their experiences, and continuously improve their skills.

Collaborative learning and interdisciplinary approaches also benefit from partnerships with external organizations and communities. Collaborations with businesses, cultural institutions, and community groups can provide students with real-world contexts for their learning, exposing them to current issues and professional practices. Internships, service-learning projects, and partnerships with industry professionals can offer valuable experiences that enhance students' academic and career development. These external collaborations can also help students see the relevance of their education to the broader world, inspiring them to apply their knowledge and skills to make a positive impact. These approaches are essential for preparing students to navigate the complexities of the modern world. By fostering teamwork, critical thinking, and the ability to integrate knowledge across disciplines, these methods enhance educational outcomes and equip students with the skills and attitudes needed for success in diverse professional environments. Implementing these approaches requires thoughtful planning, supportive learning environments, innovative assessment methods, and partnerships with external organizations. By embracing collaborative and interdisciplinary learning, educators can create dynamic, inclusive, and engaging educational experiences that prepare students to thrive in an interconnected and rapidly changing world.

Chapter 2: In-Demand Skills and Certifications

The rapid proliferation of artificial intelligence (AI) and related technologies is transforming the landscape of the job market, creating a pressing need for individuals to continuously update their skills and qualifications. As we move deeper into the AI era, the skills that are in high demand are evolving rapidly, driven by technological advancements and changing industry needs. In this dynamic environment, understanding which skills are most sought after and how to acquire them is crucial for career advancement and long-term employability.

Identifying high-demand skills in the AI era requires an understanding of both current and emerging trends. AI and machine learning (ML) are at the forefront of this transformation, making skills in these areas highly valuable. Professionals with expertise in AI and ML can design algorithms, build predictive models, and analyze large datasets, enabling businesses to harness the power of data for strategic decision-making. Additionally, skills in data science, data analytics, and big data are essential, as they complement AI technologies by allowing organizations to extract meaningful insights from vast amounts of information. Knowledge of programming languages such as Python, R, and Java, as well as proficiency in using AI frameworks and tools, is also highly sought after.

Beyond AI-specific skills, there is a growing demand for expertise in cybersecurity. As digital transformation accelerates, the need to protect sensitive information from cyber threats becomes increasingly critical. Professionals skilled in cybersecurity can design robust security architectures, identify and mitigate vulnerabilities, and ensure the integrity and confidentiality of data. Furthermore, cloud computing skills are essential, as more organizations migrate their operations to the cloud. Proficiency in cloud platforms such as Amazon Web Services (AWS), Microsoft Azure, and Google Cloud Platform (GCP) is highly valued, as these skills enable businesses to leverage the scalability, flexibility, and cost-efficiency of cloud technologies.

The role of certifications and micro-credentials in career advancement cannot be overstated in this context. Traditional degrees and long-term educational programs, while still important, are often insufficient to keep pace with the rapid changes in technology and industry demands. Certifications and micro-credentials offer a more agile and focused approach to skill development, allowing individuals to gain recognized qualifications in specific areas quickly. These credentials provide tangible proof of expertise, making it easier for employers to assess the competencies of potential hires. Certifications from reputable organizations, such as CompTIA, Cisco, and (ISC)² in cybersecurity, or AWS, Microsoft, and Google in cloud computing, are particularly valuable. They signal to employers that an individual possesses the necessary skills and knowledge to perform effectively in their role.

Popular upskilling and reskilling programs are also instrumental in helping professionals stay relevant in the AI era. Upskilling involves enhancing existing skills, while reskilling focuses on acquiring new skills to transition into different roles or industries. Many educational institutions, online platforms, and industry organizations offer programs tailored to the needs of the modern workforce. For instance, massive open online courses (MOOCs) from providers like Coursera, edX, and Udacity offer a wide range of courses in AI, data science, and other high-demand fields. These platforms provide flexible learning options, allowing individuals to study at their own pace and balance their education with other commitments. Corporate training programs and bootcamps are also popular, offering intensive, hands-on training that equips participants with practical skills in a relatively short time.

Industry-specific skill requirements vary, reflecting the unique demands and challenges of different sectors. In healthcare, for example, there is a growing need for professionals skilled in health informatics, telemedicine, and medical data analysis. These skills enable the integration of AI technologies to improve patient care, streamline administrative processes, and enhance medical research. In finance, expertise in fintech, blockchain, and quantitative analysis is crucial, as these skills drive innovations in banking, investment, and financial services. The manufacturing sector, on the other hand, increasingly relies on skills in robotics, automation, and industrial IoT (Internet of Things) to optimize production processes and improve operational efficiency.

The importance of technical and non-technical skills cannot be overlooked in the AI era. While technical skills are essential for developing and implementing AI technologies, non-technical skills play a critical role in ensuring their effective application and integration within organizations. Critical thinking, problem-solving, and creativity are vital, as they enable professionals to tackle complex challenges, generate innovative solutions, and drive continuous improvement. Communication skills are equally important, as they facilitate collaboration and knowledge sharing among diverse teams. The ability to articulate technical concepts to non-technical stakeholders is particularly valuable, as it ensures that everyone within the organization understands the implications and benefits of AI initiatives.

Emotional intelligence, adaptability, and leadership are also crucial non-technical skills. Emotional intelligence helps professionals navigate interpersonal dynamics, build strong working relationships, and lead teams effectively. Adaptability is essential in a rapidly changing environment, enabling individuals to embrace new technologies, processes, and roles with resilience and agility. Leadership skills are important at all levels, as they inspire and motivate teams, foster a culture of innovation, and drive strategic initiatives that leverage AI and other advanced technologies.

Identifying high-demand skills in the AI era requires a keen understanding of both current trends and emerging technologies. The rapid integration of AI across various industries has created a surge in demand for specific skill sets that enable professionals to develop, manage, and utilize AI systems effectively. At the forefront of these in-demand skills are AI and machine learning (ML). Professionals with expertise in AI and ML can design sophisticated algorithms, build predictive models, and analyze vast amounts of data to extract valuable insights. This capability is crucial for businesses looking to leverage AI for strategic decision-making and operational efficiency. Proficiency in programming languages such as Python, R, and Java, along with familiarity with AI frameworks like TensorFlow and PyTorch, is highly sought after, as these tools are foundational for creating AI applications.

Data science and data analytics are other critical areas where skills are in high demand. The ability to analyze large datasets and derive actionable insights is essential for organizations aiming to make data-driven decisions. Data scientists and analysts use statistical techniques and software tools to interpret complex data sets, identify trends, and inform business strategies. Their work is pivotal in industries ranging from healthcare and finance to retail and technology, where data-driven insights can drive innovation and competitive advantage. Skills in data visualization tools, such as Tableau and Power BI, are also valuable, as they help in presenting data insights in an understandable and impactful manner.

Cybersecurity has emerged as a crucial area of expertise due to the increasing threats to digital information. As more business operations move online and data breaches become more frequent, the need for robust cybersecurity measures has never been greater. Professionals skilled in cybersecurity are responsible for designing and implementing security protocols, identifying and mitigating vulnerabilities, and ensuring the protection of sensitive data. Knowledge of security frameworks, encryption techniques, and compliance standards is vital, along with hands-on experience with security tools and platforms.

Cloud computing is another area where skills are in high demand. As organizations continue to migrate their infrastructure to the cloud to take advantage of its scalability, flexibility, and cost-efficiency, expertise in cloud platforms like Amazon Web Services (AWS), Microsoft Azure, and Google Cloud Platform (GCP) becomes increasingly valuable. Professionals with cloud computing skills can architect, deploy, and manage cloud-based solutions, ensuring that organizations can leverage the full potential of cloud technology.

In addition to these technical skills, there is a growing recognition of the importance of soft skills in the AI era. Critical thinking, problem-solving, and creativity are essential for tackling the complex challenges that come with implementing and managing AI technologies. These skills enable professionals to approach problems from multiple perspectives, generate innovative solutions, and continuously improve processes and systems. Effective communication skills are equally important, as they facilitate collaboration within teams and help in conveying technical concepts to non-technical stakeholders. The ability to translate complex technical details into understandable and actionable information is crucial for ensuring that AI initiatives are aligned with business goals and objectives.

Emotional intelligence and adaptability are also increasingly valued. Emotional intelligence helps professionals manage interpersonal relationships, navigate the complexities of team dynamics, and lead with empathy and understanding. Adaptability is vital in an environment characterized by rapid technological change, allowing individuals to quickly learn new skills, embrace new tools and technologies, and adjust to new roles and responsibilities.

In the fast-paced and ever-evolving landscape of the AI era, traditional educational pathways alone often cannot keep up with the rapid development of new technologies and industry requirements. This is where certifications and micro-credentials play a crucial role in career advancement. These forms of credentialing provide targeted, up-to-date, and flexible learning opportunities that allow individuals to quickly acquire and demonstrate specific skills and knowledge pertinent to their fields.

Certifications offer a way for professionals to validate their expertise in particular areas, whether it's in cloud computing, cybersecurity, data science, or AI and machine learning. Issued by reputable organizations and industry leaders, these certifications signal to employers that a candidate possesses the necessary skills and knowledge to perform effectively. For example, certifications from tech giants like Amazon Web Services (AWS), Microsoft Azure, and Google Cloud Platform (GCP) are highly regarded in the field of cloud computing. Similarly, cybersecurity certifications from organizations such as CompTIA, Cisco, and (ISC)² carry significant weight and are often prerequisites for advanced roles in the industry.

Micro-credentials, on the other hand, are smaller, more focused certifications that cover specific skills or knowledge areas within a broader field. They provide a flexible and modular approach to learning, allowing professionals to build their expertise incrementally. Micro-credentials can be particularly beneficial for individuals looking to pivot to new roles or industries, as they can quickly gain the foundational skills needed to make such transitions. For instance, a software developer looking to move into data science might start with micro-credentials in data analysis and machine learning before pursuing more comprehensive certifications.

The flexibility of certifications and micro-credentials is one of their most significant advantages. They can often be completed online, at one's own pace, making them accessible to working professionals who need to balance their education with other commitments. This accessibility enables continuous learning and skill development, which is essential in a rapidly changing job market. Employers value these credentials because they provide assurance that the holder has up-to-date knowledge and skills, which is particularly important in fields where technology and best practices evolve quickly.

Certifications and micro-credentials often include practical, hands-on components that ensure learners can apply what they've learned in real-world scenarios. This practical experience is invaluable, as it bridges the gap between theoretical knowledge and actual job performance. By completing projects, case studies, or simulations as part of their certification process, professionals can demonstrate their ability to tackle real-world challenges, which can be a significant differentiator in the job market. In addition to enhancing technical skills, certifications and micro-credentials can also help professionals develop soft skills that are crucial for career advancement. Many programs include components on leadership, communication, and project management, recognizing that these skills are essential for effectively implementing technical solutions and leading teams. This holistic approach to professional development ensures that individuals are well-rounded and capable of contributing to their organizations in multiple ways.

Employers often support certification and micro-credentialing programs because they align with organizational goals of maintaining a highly skilled and adaptable workforce. Investing in employee development through these programs can lead to higher productivity, improved job performance, and increased employee retention. For employees, obtaining certifications and micro-credentials can lead to career advancement opportunities, higher salaries, and greater job satisfaction.

In the face of rapid technological advancements and shifting industry demands, upskilling and reskilling programs have become crucial for maintaining employability and ensuring career growth. These programs are designed to help individuals enhance their current skill sets or acquire new skills to transition into different roles or industries, thereby addressing the evolving needs of the modern workforce.

One of the most popular forms of upskilling and reskilling is through massive open online courses (MOOCs). Platforms such as Coursera, edX, and Udacity offer a vast array of courses covering a wide range of subjects, including AI, data science, programming, cybersecurity, and digital marketing. These platforms collaborate with leading universities and industry experts to provide high-quality education that is accessible to learners worldwide. The flexibility of MOOCs allows individuals to learn at their own pace and on their own schedule, making it easier to balance education with professional and personal commitments. Many of these courses also offer certificates upon completion, which can be valuable additions to a professional's resume.

Corporate training programs are another effective avenue for upskilling and reskilling. Many companies recognize the importance of continuous learning and invest in training programs to ensure their employees stay current with industry trends and technologies. These programs often include workshops, seminars, and hands-on training sessions tailored to the specific needs of the organization. By providing employees with opportunities to develop new skills, companies can foster a culture of innovation and adaptability, which is essential for staying competitive in the marketplace.

Bootcamps have gained popularity as intensive, short-term training programs that focus on specific skills, particularly in tech-related fields. Coding bootcamps, for instance, offer immersive training in software development, teaching participants how to code and build applications in a matter of weeks. These programs are designed to be highly practical, with a strong emphasis on real-world projects and collaboration. Graduates of coding bootcamps often find themselves well-prepared for entry-level positions in tech companies, making bootcamps a viable option for those looking to make a career change quickly.

Professional associations and industry organizations also play a significant role in upskilling and reskilling efforts. These organizations offer certification programs, workshops, and conferences that provide members with the latest knowledge and best practices in their fields. For example, the Project Management Institute (PMI) offers certifications that are widely recognized in the field of project management, while the International Information System Security Certification Consortium (ISC)² provides certifications for cybersecurity professionals. By participating in these programs, individuals can stay abreast of industry developments and enhance their professional credentials.

Community colleges and vocational schools offer a variety of upskilling and reskilling programs that are often more affordable and accessible than traditional four-year degrees. These institutions provide courses and certifications in areas such as healthcare, information technology, advanced manufacturing, and skilled trades. Community colleges also often partner with local businesses to create programs that are aligned with regional labor market needs, ensuring that graduates have the skills required by local employers.

In-house training programs developed by companies for their employees are another effective method of upskilling and reskilling. These programs are tailored to the specific needs of the organization and can include a range of learning opportunities, from on-the-job training and mentorship to formal classes and online courses. In-house training ensures that employees acquire skills that are directly relevant to their roles and the company's strategic goals, fostering a more capable and cohesive workforce.

Industry-specific skill requirements are becoming increasingly vital as technological advancements and market demands evolve. Different sectors have unique needs and challenges, necessitating specialized knowledge and competencies for professionals within those fields. In healthcare, for example, there is a growing demand for skills in health informatics, telemedicine, and medical data analysis. These abilities enable the integration of AI technologies to improve patient care, streamline administrative processes, and enhance medical research. Professionals in this industry must be adept at using electronic health records (EHRs), understanding data privacy regulations, and applying data analytics to clinical decision-making.

The finance sector, on the other hand, requires expertise in fintech, blockchain, and quantitative analysis. As financial services increasingly rely on digital transactions and sophisticated data analytics, professionals must be proficient in managing digital currencies, ensuring cybersecurity, and employing algorithmic trading. Knowledge of regulatory frameworks and risk management is also critical to navigate the complex financial landscape.

In the field of manufacturing, skills in robotics, automation, and industrial Internet of Things (IoT) are highly sought after. The push towards smart manufacturing and Industry 4.0 necessitates expertise in programming and maintaining automated systems, analyzing production data for efficiency improvements, and integrating IoT devices to monitor and control industrial processes. Professionals must be capable of troubleshooting complex machinery and optimizing production workflows to enhance productivity and reduce downtime.

The retail industry, increasingly driven by e-commerce and digital marketing, demands skills in customer relationship management (CRM), data-driven marketing strategies, and supply chain optimization. Professionals in this field must be adept at utilizing big data analytics to understand consumer behavior, managing online sales platforms, and developing personalized marketing campaigns. Additionally, supply chain expertise is crucial for managing logistics, inventory, and distribution in a highly competitive market.

In the realm of education, there is a growing emphasis on skills in educational technology, online pedagogy, and curriculum development for digital learning environments. Educators must be proficient in using learning management systems (LMS), creating engaging online content, and employing data analytics to assess student performance and improve instructional strategies. Understanding the principles of digital literacy and fostering an inclusive learning environment are also essential components of modern education.

The energy sector, particularly with the rise of renewable energy sources, requires skills in sustainable energy technologies, environmental impact assessment, and smart grid management. Professionals must be knowledgeable about the latest advancements in solar, wind, and other renewable energy technologies, as well as adept at managing energy storage systems and optimizing energy distribution networks. Environmental regulations and sustainability practices are critical areas of expertise for ensuring compliance and promoting eco-friendly initiatives.

In the technology industry itself, skills in software development, cybersecurity, and cloud computing are paramount. Software developers must be proficient in various programming languages and development frameworks, capable of building scalable and secure applications. Cybersecurity experts need to stay ahead of emerging threats, implementing robust security measures and conducting thorough risk assessments. Cloud computing professionals must be skilled in managing cloud infrastructure, optimizing cloud resources, and ensuring the security and reliability of cloud services.

The automotive industry, with its shift towards electric vehicles (EVs) and autonomous driving technologies, requires expertise in battery technology, electrical engineering, and machine learning. Professionals must be capable of designing and optimizing battery systems, developing autonomous driving algorithms, and integrating AI technologies into vehicle systems for improved safety and efficiency.

In the rapidly evolving landscape of the modern workforce, the importance of both technical and non-technical skills cannot be overstated. As technology continues to advance and permeate various aspects of work and daily life, possessing a balanced skill set that includes both technical expertise and essential soft skills is crucial for career success and adaptability.

Technical skills, often referred to as hard skills, are specific abilities and knowledge required to perform particular tasks. These skills are typically acquired through formal education, training programs, and hands-on experience. In the context of the AI era, technical skills such as programming, data analysis, machine learning, and cybersecurity are in high demand.

Proficiency in programming languages like Python, R, and Java, as well as familiarity with AI frameworks and tools, is essential for developing and implementing AI solutions. Similarly, expertise in data science and analytics enables professionals to interpret complex datasets and derive actionable insights, which are critical for informed decision-making in various industries. Cybersecurity skills are vital for protecting sensitive information and ensuring the integrity of digital systems in an increasingly interconnected world. However, technical skills alone are not sufficient for long-term success and growth. Non-technical skills, or soft skills, play an equally important role in professional development and organizational effectiveness. These skills encompass interpersonal abilities, communication, emotional intelligence, problem-solving, and adaptability. In a collaborative work environment, strong communication skills are necessary for effectively conveying ideas, facilitating teamwork, and building relationships with colleagues and clients. The ability to articulate complex technical concepts to non-technical stakeholders is particularly valuable, as it ensures alignment and understanding across different parts of an organization.

Emotional intelligence, which involves the ability to recognize and manage one's own emotions as well as understand and influence the emotions of others, is crucial for leadership and teamwork. Professionals with high emotional intelligence can navigate interpersonal dynamics, resolve conflicts, and foster a positive work environment. This skill is essential for creating a collaborative and inclusive workplace culture, where diverse perspectives are valued and innovation thrives.

Problem-solving skills are fundamental in the AI era, where challenges and opportunities often require creative and strategic thinking. The ability to analyze situations, identify underlying issues, and develop innovative solutions is critical for addressing complex problems that do not have straightforward answers. This skill set enables professionals to approach challenges from multiple angles, consider various possibilities, and implement effective strategies.

Adaptability is another key non-technical skill, particularly in a world characterized by rapid change and uncertainty. The ability to quickly learn new technologies, adjust to evolving roles, and remain resilient in the face of setbacks is essential for staying relevant and competitive. Adaptable professionals are better equipped to embrace new opportunities and navigate the shifting demands of the job market.

Leadership skills, encompassing both technical and non-technical abilities, are vital for guiding teams and organizations through the complexities of the modern business environment. Effective leaders inspire and motivate their teams, drive strategic initiatives, and foster a culture of continuous learning and innovation. They must balance technical knowledge with the ability to manage people, communicate effectively, and make ethical decisions.

Chapter 3: Lifelong Learning and Continuous Development

In an era defined by rapid technological advancements and constant change, the concept of lifelong learning and continuous development has never been more critical. The traditional model of education, which once relied on completing formal education early in life and applying that knowledge throughout a career, is now outdated. Instead, the modern professional landscape demands a commitment to ongoing education and skill development. This chapter explores the essential elements of lifelong learning and continuous development, emphasizing the need for individuals to remain active learners throughout their lives to stay relevant and competitive in the job market.

Being an active lifelong learner is no longer optional; it is a necessity. The pace at which new technologies and methodologies emerge means that the knowledge and skills acquired during formal education can quickly become obsolete. To adapt to this reality, individuals must embrace a mindset that values continuous learning and self-improvement. This proactive approach to education not only enhances employability but also fosters personal growth and fulfillment. By continually seeking new knowledge and skills, individuals can remain agile and adaptable, better prepared to meet the challenges and opportunities of an ever-changing world.

Effective self-directed learning strategies are crucial for sustaining lifelong learning. Self-directed learners take charge of their educational journey, setting their own goals, identifying resources, and managing their time effectively. This chapter delves into various strategies that can help individuals become successful self-directed learners. These strategies include setting clear, achievable goals, developing a structured learning plan, and utilizing a variety of learning methods to maintain engagement and motivation. By mastering these techniques, individuals can tailor their learning experiences to their personal and professional needs, ensuring they continue to grow and evolve.

Utilizing online resources and educational platforms is another key aspect of lifelong learning. The internet has revolutionized access to information, providing a wealth of resources that can support continuous development. Online courses, webinars, podcasts, and educational videos offer flexible and convenient ways to acquire new knowledge and skills. Platforms such as Coursera, edX, and Udacity provide access to courses from top universities and industry experts, allowing learners to study at their own pace and on their own schedule. This chapter highlights the importance of leveraging these digital tools to enhance one's learning journey, making education more accessible and adaptable to individual needs.

Balancing formal and informal learning opportunities is essential for comprehensive development. Formal education, such as degree programs and professional certifications, provides structured learning and recognized credentials that can enhance career prospects. However, informal learning, which includes self-study, on-the-job training, and experiential learning, is equally important. This chapter explores how to effectively integrate both types of learning to create a well-rounded educational experience. By combining formal education with informal learning opportunities, individuals can gain a deeper understanding of their fields and develop practical skills that are immediately applicable in the workplace.

Building a personal learning network is a powerful way to support lifelong learning. A personal learning network consists of individuals, resources, and tools that facilitate ongoing education and professional development. This network can include mentors, colleagues, industry experts, and online communities. By actively engaging with a diverse learning network, individuals can stay informed about the latest trends and best practices in their field, receive valuable feedback and guidance, and find inspiration and support. This chapter provides insights into how to build and maintain a robust personal learning network, emphasizing the importance of collaboration and knowledge sharing.

In today's rapidly evolving professional landscape, the necessity of being an active lifelong learner is paramount. The pace of technological advancements, industry transformations, and the continuous emergence of new knowledge mean that the skills and expertise acquired during formal education can quickly become outdated. To remain relevant and competitive, individuals must commit to ongoing education and skill development throughout their careers.

Being an active lifelong learner involves a proactive approach to personal and professional growth. It means continuously seeking new knowledge, skills, and experiences that can enhance one's abilities and adapt to changing job market demands. This proactive learning is not just about keeping up with the latest trends but about anticipating future developments and preparing for new opportunities and challenges.

The necessity for lifelong learning is underscored by the increasing complexity and interdisciplinarity of modern work. Professionals are often required to integrate knowledge from various fields, solve complex problems, and innovate within their roles. This requires a diverse skill set and a broad understanding of different disciplines, which can only be achieved through continuous learning. Lifelong learners are better equipped to think critically, adapt to new technologies, and apply their knowledge in novel ways, making them invaluable assets to any organization.

The modern job market is characterized by frequent changes in job roles and career paths. Traditional career trajectories, where individuals remain in the same job or industry for their entire careers, are becoming less common. Instead, professionals are increasingly expected to pivot to new roles, learn new skills, and adapt to different work environments throughout their careers. This fluidity demands a mindset geared toward lifelong learning, where individuals are always ready to acquire new competencies and embrace new opportunities.

The necessity of being an active lifelong learner also extends to personal growth and fulfillment. Engaging in continuous learning can lead to a greater sense of achievement, confidence, and satisfaction. It allows individuals to explore their interests, pursue their passions, and develop a deeper understanding of the world around them. This personal enrichment not only enhances professional capabilities but also contributes to overall well-being and happiness.

Lifelong learning fosters resilience and adaptability, essential qualities in an unpredictable and rapidly changing world. The ability to learn and adapt quickly to new situations helps individuals navigate career disruptions, economic shifts, and technological changes more effectively. Lifelong learners are more likely to embrace change as an opportunity rather than a threat, positioning themselves to thrive in dynamic environments.

Employers increasingly recognize the value of lifelong learning and actively seek individuals who demonstrate a commitment to continuous development. Organizations that foster a culture of learning and provide opportunities for professional growth are more likely to attract and retain top talent. By investing in lifelong learning, both employees and employers can benefit from increased innovation, productivity, and competitiveness.

Effective self-directed learning strategies are crucial for lifelong learners who aim to stay relevant and competitive in today's rapidly evolving professional landscape. These strategies enable individuals to take charge of their educational journey, tailoring their learning experiences to their personal and professional needs.

Setting clear, achievable goals is fundamental to self-directed learning. Goals provide direction and motivation, helping learners focus their efforts and measure their progress. It's important to set both short-term and long-term goals that are specific, measurable, attainable, relevant, and time-bound (SMART). By breaking down larger objectives into smaller, manageable tasks, learners can maintain momentum and achieve their goals incrementally.

Developing a structured learning plan helps organize the learning process and ensures that time is used effectively. A learning plan should outline what will be learned, the resources needed, and the timeline for completion. This plan acts as a roadmap, guiding learners through their educational journey and helping them stay on track. Regularly reviewing and adjusting the plan is important to accommodate new interests, goals, or unforeseen challenges.

Utilizing a variety of learning methods keeps the learning process engaging and caters to different learning styles. Combining reading, watching videos, participating in online courses, attending workshops, and engaging in hands-on projects can enhance understanding and retention. Experimenting with different methods also allows learners to discover which techniques work best for them, making their learning experience more effective and enjoyable.

Leveraging online resources and educational platforms is essential in the digital age. Platforms like Coursera, edX, Udacity, and Khan Academy offer a wide range of courses across various subjects, often taught by experts from leading institutions. These platforms provide flexibility, allowing learners to study at their own pace and access high-quality materials from anywhere. Additionally, resources like YouTube, podcasts, and educational blogs can supplement learning and provide diverse perspectives on a topic.

Engaging with a learning community enhances the self-directed learning experience by providing support, feedback, and opportunities for collaboration. Joining online forums, study groups, or professional networks allows learners to connect with others who share similar interests and goals. Participating in discussions, asking questions, and sharing insights can deepen understanding and foster a sense of accountability and motivation.

Reflecting on the learning process and outcomes is a critical strategy for self-directed learners. Regular reflection helps learners evaluate their progress, identify areas for improvement, and reinforce what they have learned. Keeping a learning journal or engaging in regular self-assessment can facilitate this reflection, enabling learners to track their achievements and adapt their strategies as needed.

Staying curious and open-minded is essential for continuous growth and development. Self-directed learners should cultivate a mindset of curiosity, always seeking to learn more and explore new topics. This openness to new ideas and experiences can lead to unexpected discoveries and a broader, more comprehensive understanding of the world.

Balancing formal and informal learning opportunities is also important for a well-rounded education. Formal learning, such as enrolling in structured courses or programs, provides a solid foundation and recognized credentials. Informal learning, which includes self-study, on-the-job training, and experiential learning, allows for flexibility and the application of knowledge in real-world contexts. Integrating both types of learning ensures a comprehensive approach to skill and knowledge development Building a personal learning network (PLN) supports self-directed learning by connecting learners with a diverse array of resources and people. A PLN can include mentors, peers, industry professionals, and digital tools that provide ongoing support and inspiration. Actively engaging with this network helps learners stay informed about the latest trends and best practices, receive valuable feedback, and gain new perspectives.

Utilizing online resources and educational platforms has become an integral part of effective self-directed learning, offering unparalleled access to knowledge and skills development. In the digital age, the internet provides a vast array of tools and platforms that cater to various learning needs and preferences, making education more accessible, flexible, and personalized.

Online educational platforms like Coursera, edX, Udacity, and Khan Academy offer a wide range of courses across diverse subjects. These platforms partner with top universities and industry experts to provide high-quality content that is both rigorous and relevant. Learners can find courses on virtually any topic, from AI and data science to humanities and business. Many of these courses are free to audit, with options to pay for certifications that can enhance one's resume and career prospects.

Massive open online courses (MOOCs) have revolutionized access to education, allowing learners to study at their own pace and schedule. This flexibility is especially beneficial for working professionals who need to balance their education with job responsibilities. MOOCs also often include interactive elements such as quizzes, peer-reviewed assignments, and discussion forums, which enhance engagement and provide opportunities for feedback and collaboration.

Specialized online platforms cater to specific skill sets and industries. For instance, platforms like Codecademy, Pluralsight, and Treehouse focus on coding and technology skills, offering hands-on practice through coding exercises and projects. For those interested in creative skills, platforms like Skillshare and CreativeLive provide courses in design, photography, writing, and more. These platforms often employ a project-based learning approach, enabling learners to apply what they've learned in practical, real-world contexts.

YouTube is another valuable resource for self-directed learners. It hosts millions of educational videos on nearly every topic imaginable, ranging from academic lectures to practical tutorials. Channels dedicated to education, such as CrashCourse, TED-Ed, and The Khan Academy, offer structured content that can supplement formal learning. The visual and auditory elements of video content can enhance understanding and retention, especially for complex subjects.

Podcasts have emerged as a popular medium for learning on the go. Educational podcasts cover a wide range of topics, providing in-depth discussions, interviews with experts, and analysis of current trends and research. Platforms like Apple Podcasts, Spotify, and Google Podcasts make it easy to find and subscribe to educational content that can be consumed during commutes, workouts, or other activities.

Online forums and communities such as Reddit, Stack Exchange, and Quora provide platforms for asking questions, sharing knowledge, and engaging in discussions with peers and experts. These communities are valuable for solving specific problems, gaining diverse perspectives, and staying updated on the latest developments in various fields. Participating in these forums can also help build a professional network and foster a sense of belonging in a community of learners.

Educational blogs and websites offer a wealth of articles, tutorials, and resources that can support self-directed learning. Websites like Medium, LinkedIn Learning, and educational institution websites provide insights and information on a wide range of topics. Following blogs and subscribing to newsletters from thought leaders and industry experts can keep learners informed about new trends, tools, and best practices.

Virtual libraries and repositories, such as Google Scholar, JSTOR, and Project Gutenberg, provide access to a vast array of academic papers, books, and research materials. These resources are invaluable for in-depth study and research, allowing learners to delve deeply into subjects of interest and support their learning with authoritative sources.

Interactive learning tools and apps, such as Duolingo for language learning, Anki for spaced repetition flashcards, and Khan Academy's personalized learning dashboard, offer engaging and effective ways to master new skills. These tools often incorporate gamification elements, making learning fun and motivating.

Building a personal learning network (PLN) is a crucial strategy for fostering continuous learning and professional development. A PLN consists of individuals, resources, and tools that provide support, knowledge, and opportunities for growth. This network can include mentors, colleagues, industry experts, and digital communities, all of which contribute to a rich, dynamic learning environment.

A key component of building a PLN is identifying and connecting with mentors. Mentors offer guidance, share their experiences, and provide valuable feedback, helping learners navigate their career paths and overcome challenges. Establishing mentor relationships can occur through formal mentorship programs, professional associations, or informal connections within one's industry. Engaging with mentors can provide insights into industry trends, career advice, and personal development strategies, making mentorship a powerful element of a PLN.

Colleagues and peers are also essential to a personal learning network. Collaborating with co-workers and peers fosters the exchange of ideas, collaborative problem-solving, and mutual support. Networking within one's organization or professional community can lead to the formation of study groups, knowledge-sharing sessions, and collaborative projects. These interactions not only enhance learning but also build a sense of community and support among professionals.

Industry experts and thought leaders play a vital role in a PLN by offering cutting-edge knowledge and insights. Following industry experts on social media, reading their blogs, attending their webinars, and engaging with their content can keep learners informed about the latest developments and best practices in their field. Engaging with thought leaders through comments, discussions, and questions can also provide opportunities for direct interaction and learning.

Digital communities and online platforms are invaluable resources for building a PLN. Platforms such as LinkedIn, Twitter, and industry-specific forums provide spaces for professionals to connect, share knowledge, and collaborate. Participating in online discussions, joining professional groups, and contributing to forums can help individuals expand their networks and gain diverse perspectives. These digital interactions can supplement face-to-face connections, making learning accessible anytime and anywhere.

Educational platforms that offer courses and learning resources often have built-in community features that facilitate networking and collaboration. Online course platforms like Coursera, edX, and Udacity include discussion forums, peer reviews, and project collaboration tools. Engaging with fellow learners on these platforms can enhance the learning experience by providing opportunities to discuss course content, share insights, and work on projects together.

Attending conferences, workshops, and seminars is another effective way to build a PLN. These events offer opportunities to meet professionals from various backgrounds, learn from industry experts, and engage in hands-on learning experiences. Networking at these events can lead to valuable connections and collaborations that extend beyond the duration of the event.

Regularly updating and maintaining a personal learning network is essential for long-term success. This involves staying active in professional communities, continuously seeking out new connections, and nurturing existing relationships. Regular engagement ensures that the network remains vibrant and responsive to the learner's evolving needs.

Building a personal learning network is a critical component of lifelong learning and continuous development. By connecting with mentors, colleagues, industry experts, and digital communities, individuals can create a robust support system that enhances their learning journey. A well-developed PLN provides access to diverse knowledge, collaborative opportunities, and ongoing support, enabling learners to stay informed, adaptable, and competitive in their professional fields. As part of a comprehensive approach to education and professional growth, a strong personal learning network is an invaluable asset in navigating the complexities and opportunities of the modern world.

Part II: Adapting to the Changing Workforce

As artificial intelligence continues to reshape the landscape of the global job market, adapting to the changing workforce becomes not just a necessity, but a critical advantage. Part II of this book, "Adapting to the Changing Workforce," delves into the practical realities and strategies required to navigate and thrive amidst these profound transformations. The dynamic nature of the modern workplace demands flexibility, resilience, and a proactive approach to both professional development and personal well-being. This section offers a comprehensive guide to understanding and embracing these changes, ensuring that individuals and organizations are well-prepared to meet the challenges and seize the opportunities presented by an AI-driven world.

The concept of a flexible workforce has gained significant traction in recent years, driven by technological advancements and shifting societal expectations. Remote work and flexible arrangements have seen exponential growth, allowing employees to work from anywhere, thereby improving productivity and job satisfaction. This chapter explores the rise of remote work, examining the benefits and challenges it presents for both employers and employees. Alongside remote work, the gig economy and freelancing opportunities have expanded, offering alternative career paths that prioritize flexibility and autonomy. These opportunities, while liberating for many, also come with unique challenges related to income stability and career development.

Maintaining work-life balance and well-being is crucial in a flexible work environment. With the blurring of boundaries between work and personal life, individuals must develop strategies to ensure they remain productive without compromising their mental and physical health. This includes setting clear boundaries, prioritizing tasks, and making time for rest and rejuvenation. The right tools and technologies play a pivotal role in facilitating flexible working arrangements. From project management software to communication platforms, these tools enable seamless collaboration and efficiency, making remote and flexible work more feasible and effective.

Legal and ethical considerations in flexible work are increasingly important as well. Employers and employees must navigate issues such as data privacy, intellectual property rights, and fair compensation. Ensuring that flexible work policies are inclusive and equitable is essential to fostering a supportive and productive work environment.

Technological disruption, driven by advancements in AI and automation, is reshaping industries and job roles at an unprecedented pace. This chapter examines the profound impact of AI on various sectors, highlighting both the opportunities and challenges it brings. As certain jobs become automated, new roles and career paths are emerging, requiring a different set of skills and competencies. Understanding these emerging job roles and preparing for them is crucial for maintaining employability in an AI-driven economy.

Cultivating a growth mindset and adaptability is essential for embracing technological disruption. A growth mindset encourages individuals to view challenges as opportunities for learning and development, rather than obstacles. This mindset, combined with adaptability, enables individuals to pivot and thrive in the face of change. Preparing for industry-specific technological changes involves staying informed about the latest advancements and trends in one's field. This proactive approach allows individuals to anticipate changes and position themselves advantageously within the evolving job market.

Mitigating risks associated with technological disruption is also a key focus of this chapter. While AI offers numerous benefits, it also poses risks such as job displacement and increased inequality. Strategies for risk mitigation include reskilling and upskilling programs, as well as policies that promote inclusive and equitable growth.

In an AI-augmented workplace, human-AI collaboration becomes increasingly important. This chapter explores how AI can complement human abilities, enhancing productivity and innovation. Successful collaboration with AI requires an understanding of its capabilities and limitations, as well as the ability to work effectively with AI tools and systems.

Enhancing communication and interpersonal skills is vital for thriving in a technologically advanced workplace. Effective communication fosters collaboration, reduces misunderstandings, and builds strong professional relationships. Developing emotional intelligence and empathy further enhances these interactions, enabling individuals to navigate complex social dynamics and support their colleagues.

Teamwork in an AI-augmented workplace is characterized by the integration of human creativity and AI efficiency. This synergy can drive innovation and improve decision-making processes. However, it also requires a shift in traditional teamwork dynamics, with an emphasis on flexibility and continuous learning.

Conflict resolution and negotiation skills are essential in a workplace where diverse perspectives and interests often intersect. These skills help individuals manage disagreements constructively and find mutually beneficial solutions, contributing to a harmonious and productive work environment.

Chapter 4: The Flexible Workforce

In recent years, the nature of work has undergone a significant transformation, driven by advancements in technology, shifting cultural attitudes, and the evolving demands of both employers and employees. One of the most profound changes has been the rise of the flexible workforce. This chapter explores the various dimensions of this new paradigm, examining how remote work, the gig economy, and flexible arrangements are reshaping the landscape of employment.

The growth of remote work and flexible arrangements has been accelerated by technological innovations that allow employees to perform their tasks from virtually anywhere. High-speed internet, cloud computing, and collaboration tools have made it possible for teams to stay connected and productive without being physically co-located. This shift has been further amplified by the global COVID-19 pandemic, which forced many organizations to adopt remote work practices out of necessity. As a result, remote work has moved from a niche arrangement to a mainstream model, with many companies embracing it as a permanent option.

Opportunities in the gig economy and freelancing have also expanded, offering workers unprecedented flexibility and autonomy. Platforms such as Uber, Upwork, and Fiverr have created new marketplaces for services, enabling individuals to offer their skills and talents on a project-by-project basis. This model of work appeals to those seeking greater control over their schedules and work-life balance, as well as to those who want to pursue multiple interests or income streams simultaneously. The gig economy has thus emerged as a viable alternative to traditional full-time employment, providing diverse opportunities for workers across various industries.

Maintaining work-life balance and well-being in a flexible work environment is crucial for sustaining productivity and job satisfaction. While flexibility offers many benefits, it can also blur the boundaries between work and personal life, leading to challenges in managing time and stress. Strategies for maintaining a healthy work-life balance include setting clear boundaries, establishing routines, and prioritizing self-care. Organizations also play a role in supporting their employees by promoting a culture that values well-being and providing resources such as mental health support and flexible scheduling options.

Tools and technologies for flexible working are essential for enabling remote work and supporting the gig economy. These include communication platforms like Slack and Microsoft Teams, project management tools such as Trello and Asana, and cloud-based storage solutions like Google Drive and Dropbox. These technologies facilitate collaboration, streamline workflows, and ensure that teams remain connected and productive regardless of their physical location. Additionally, cybersecurity tools are critical for protecting sensitive information and maintaining the integrity of digital workspaces.

Legal and ethical considerations in flexible work are increasingly important as the nature of employment evolves. Issues such as employee classification, labor rights, data privacy, and equitable treatment must be addressed to ensure that flexible work arrangements are fair and sustainable. Employers need to navigate the complexities of labor laws and regulations to avoid misclassifying workers and to provide appropriate benefits and protections. Ethical considerations also include fostering an inclusive work environment and ensuring that all employees, regardless of their work arrangement, have access to opportunities for growth and development.

The growth of remote work and flexible arrangements created by companies marks a transformative shift in the traditional employment landscape. This evolution has been driven by a confluence of technological advancements, changing workforce expectations, and, more recently, the global COVID-19 pandemic, which has accelerated the adoption of these practices on an unprecedented scale.

Initially, remote work was often seen as a perk offered by forward-thinking companies to attract and retain talent. However, as high-speed internet, cloud computing, and collaboration tools such as Slack, Zoom, and Microsoft Teams became more ubiquitous and sophisticated, the feasibility and efficiency of remote work became undeniable. These technologies have enabled employees to communicate and collaborate seamlessly, regardless of their physical location, thus maintaining productivity and team cohesion.

The pandemic forced companies worldwide to rapidly adapt to remote work models to ensure business continuity. Organizations that had previously resisted or only dabbled in remote work found themselves compelled to implement these arrangements broadly. This sudden shift revealed that many jobs could be performed just as effectively outside traditional office settings. Consequently, many companies have embraced remote work as a permanent fixture, recognizing its potential for cost savings on office space, reduced commuting time for employees, and the ability to tap into a broader talent pool unrestricted by geographical boundaries.

Flexible work arrangements extend beyond remote work to include various models such as hybrid work schedules, compressed workweeks, flextime, and job sharing. Hybrid models, which combine remote and on-site work, have gained particular traction. They offer the benefits of remote work, such as increased autonomy and work-life balance, while still providing opportunities for in-person collaboration and team building. Compressed workweeks allow employees to work the same number of hours over fewer days, providing longer periods of rest and recovery. Flextime enables workers to adjust their start and end times to better accommodate personal commitments, thereby enhancing overall job satisfaction and productivity.

Companies implementing these flexible arrangements have seen numerous benefits. Employee satisfaction and engagement often increase when individuals have greater control over their work schedules and environments. This autonomy can lead to higher productivity, as employees are able to work during their most productive hours and minimize time lost to commuting. Additionally, flexible work arrangements can reduce overhead costs for companies, as they require less office space and resources.

However, the shift to remote work and flexible arrangements is not without challenges. Companies must address issues such as maintaining team cohesion and company culture in a dispersed workforce. Regular virtual meetings, team-building activities, and effective communication strategies are essential to keep employees connected and engaged. Furthermore, managing remote teams requires new approaches to performance measurement and accountability, emphasizing outcomes rather than hours spent in the office.

Data security and privacy also become more critical as employees access company systems from various locations. Companies need to implement robust cybersecurity measures to protect sensitive information and ensure compliance with data protection regulations. Providing employees with secure devices, VPN access, and training on cybersecurity best practices is crucial to safeguarding company data.

The legal and regulatory landscape is another area that companies must navigate carefully. Remote work can complicate issues related to labor laws, taxation, and employee benefits, especially when employees are working from different states or countries. Employers need to stay informed about relevant regulations and adapt their policies to ensure compliance.

The gig economy and freelancing have opened up a wealth of opportunities for workers, offering unparalleled flexibility, autonomy, and the potential for diverse income streams. This evolving landscape is characterized by short-term contracts, project-based work, and independent contracting, facilitated by digital platforms that connect freelancers with clients worldwide.

For many, the allure of the gig economy lies in the flexibility it offers. Freelancers and gig workers have the freedom to choose their projects, set their own schedules, and work from virtually any location. This autonomy allows individuals to balance work with personal commitments, pursue multiple interests, and create a work-life balance that suits their needs.

The gig economy enables workers to diversify their income sources by taking on multiple projects or gigs simultaneously. This diversification can provide financial stability and reduce dependence on a single employer. Freelancers can leverage their skills in various industries, tapping into different markets and client bases. Moreover, gig work provides opportunities for continuous learning and skill development. By working on a variety of projects with different clients, freelancers can acquire new skills, gain experience in multiple fields, and stay current with industry trends. This varied experience can enhance their professional portfolio, making them more attractive to future clients and employers.

Digital platforms like Upwork, Fiverr, and Freelancer have revolutionized the way freelancers connect with clients. These platforms provide access to a global marketplace, allowing freelancers to offer their services to clients from around the world. This international reach can lead to more job opportunities, higher earning potential, and exposure to diverse work experiences. The gig economy also fosters an entrepreneurial spirit, enabling individuals to build their own businesses and personal brands. Freelancers have the opportunity to market their unique skills and services, establish a client base, and grow their businesses on their own terms. This entrepreneurial approach can lead to greater job satisfaction and financial independence.

Freelancers have the flexibility to specialize in niche markets or focus on specific skill sets that are in high demand. This specialization can lead to higher rates of compensation and the ability to become an expert in a particular field. Niche markets often have less competition, allowing freelancers to establish themselves as go-to professionals in their areas of expertise.

Additionally, gig work offers a diverse range of projects, allowing freelancers to explore different industries, roles, and creative opportunities. This variety can keep work engaging and prevent burnout. Freelancers can choose projects that align with their interests and passions, making their work more fulfilling and enjoyable. Freelancers have the potential to scale their businesses by taking on more clients, increasing their rates, or hiring subcontractors to handle additional work. This scalability allows freelancers to grow their income and expand their operations over time. Successful freelancers can transition into small business owners, managing larger teams and more complex projects. The gig economy also provides ample opportunities for networking and building professional relationships. Freelancers often collaborate with various clients, peers, and industry professionals, creating a broad network of contacts. These connections can lead to future job opportunities, partnerships, and referrals, enhancing career prospects.

The flexibility and autonomy of gig work contribute to a better work-life balance and higher job satisfaction. Freelancers can tailor their work schedules to fit their personal lives, reducing stress and increasing overall well-being. The ability to choose projects that align with personal values and interests also contributes to greater job satisfaction. The gig economy and freelancing offer numerous opportunities for individuals seeking flexibility, autonomy, and diverse income streams. By leveraging digital platforms, specializing in niche markets, and continuously developing their skills, freelancers can build successful and fulfilling careers. The evolving nature of work in the gig economy presents a dynamic and promising landscape for those willing to embrace its potential.

Maintaining work-life balance and well-being in the gig economy and flexible work environments requires intentional strategies and a deep understanding of one's personal and professional needs. For many freelancers and remote workers, the freedom to set their schedules and work from anywhere is both a blessing and a challenge. Without the traditional boundaries of a nine-to-five job, it's easy for work to spill into personal time, leading to stress and burnout. However, with mindful practices, individuals can achieve a harmonious balance that promotes both productivity and personal fulfillment.

One key to maintaining work-life balance is setting clear boundaries. Freelancers and remote workers should establish specific work hours and stick to them as much as possible. This means defining a start and end time for the workday and communicating these boundaries to clients and colleagues. By doing so, they can create a structured routine that delineates when work begins and ends, helping to prevent work from encroaching on personal time. Additionally, having a designated workspace, even if it's just a corner of a room, can help create a physical boundary that signals when it's time to work and when it's time to relax.

Regular breaks are essential for maintaining mental and physical health. Freelancers can incorporate short breaks throughout the day to step away from their screens, stretch, and refresh their minds. Techniques such as the Pomodoro Technique, which involves working for a set period (like 25 minutes) followed by a short break, can enhance focus and prevent fatigue. Longer breaks, such as a lunch break or a walk outside, can also provide a much-needed respite and help sustain energy levels throughout the day.

Prioritizing self-care is crucial for sustaining long-term well-being. This includes engaging in regular physical activity, maintaining a healthy diet, and getting adequate sleep. Exercise, in particular, has been shown to reduce stress, improve mood, and increase overall energy levels. Freelancers should schedule regular workouts or physical activities that they enjoy, whether it's yoga, running, or simply walking in nature. Healthy eating habits and sufficient sleep are equally important, as they directly impact cognitive function, mood, and resilience.

Mindfulness and relaxation techniques can also play a significant role in managing stress and maintaining well-being. Practices such as meditation, deep breathing exercises, and mindfulness can help individuals stay grounded and focused, reducing anxiety and enhancing overall mental health. Setting aside a few minutes each day for mindfulness practices can make a substantial difference in how one handles the pressures of work and life.

Social connections are another critical aspect of well-being that should not be neglected. Working remotely or freelancing can sometimes feel isolating, so it's important to make an effort to stay connected with friends, family, and professional networks. Regular social interactions, whether through virtual meetings, phone calls, or in-person gatherings, can provide emotional support, reduce feelings of isolation, and contribute to a sense of community and belonging.

Effective time management is key to balancing work and personal life. Freelancers should prioritize their tasks, set realistic goals, and use tools like to-do lists or digital planners to organize their workload. By breaking down larger projects into manageable tasks and setting deadlines, they can maintain a steady workflow without feeling overwhelmed. Additionally, learning to say no to projects that are not aligned with their goals or that could lead to overcommitment is an important skill for maintaining balance. Lastly, seeking support when needed is crucial. Whether it's professional coaching, therapy, or joining support groups for freelancers, having access to resources and guidance can help individuals navigate the challenges of maintaining work-life balance. Professional help can provide strategies for managing stress, improving productivity, and enhancing overall well-being.

Tools and technologies have become indispensable in enabling flexible working, allowing individuals and teams to remain productive and connected regardless of their physical locations. One of the most transformative tools for flexible work is communication platforms. Applications like Slack and Microsoft Teams facilitate instant messaging, video conferencing, and collaboration, enabling teams to communicate in real-time, share updates, and collaborate on projects seamlessly. These platforms often integrate with other tools, creating a centralized hub where work happens, reducing the need for constant email exchanges and making it easier to track conversations and project progress.

Project management tools are another cornerstone of flexible working. Platforms such as Trello, Asana, and Monday.com provide robust solutions for managing tasks, deadlines, and team responsibilities. These tools allow users to create project boards, assign tasks, set deadlines, and monitor progress in a visual and organized manner. The ability to see the status of projects at a glance helps teams stay aligned and ensures that everyone is aware of their responsibilities and timelines. This transparency and accountability are crucial for maintaining productivity in a dispersed work environment.

Cloud storage solutions like Google Drive, Dropbox, and OneDrive have revolutionized the way documents and files are stored and accessed. These platforms allow users to store files in the cloud, making them accessible from any device with an internet connection. Collaboration is made simple through shared folders and real-time editing capabilities, where multiple users can work on the same document simultaneously. This functionality eliminates the challenges associated with file version control and ensures that everyone has access to the most up-to-date information.

Video conferencing tools, such as Zoom and Google Meet, have become essential for remote meetings, webinars, and virtual collaborations. These platforms provide high-quality video and audio capabilities, along with features like screen sharing, recording, and breakout rooms for smaller group discussions. Video conferencing helps replicate the face-to-face interaction that is often missing in remote work, fostering better communication and engagement among team members.

Time management and productivity tools are also crucial for flexible working. Applications like Toggl, RescueTime, and Focus@Will help individuals track their time, understand their work patterns, and optimize their productivity. These tools provide insights into how time is spent on different tasks and projects, enabling workers to make data-driven decisions about how to manage their time more effectively. Additionally, tools that block distracting websites or create focused work sessions can help maintain concentration and efficiency.

Cybersecurity tools play a vital role in ensuring that remote work environments are secure. Virtual Private Networks (VPNs) like NordVPN and ExpressVPN provide secure connections to the internet, protecting sensitive data from potential threats. Antivirus software and firewalls add additional layers of security, while password managers like LastPass and 1Password help users create and store strong passwords securely. These tools are essential for protecting company data and maintaining the integrity of digital workspaces. Lastly, collaborative document editing tools such as Google Docs and Microsoft Office 365 enable teams to work together on documents, spreadsheets, and presentations in real-time. These platforms support collaborative writing, editing, and commenting, making it easier for teams to develop and refine content together. The ability to see changes as they happen and to revert to previous versions if needed ensures a smooth and efficient collaborative process.

The rise of flexible work arrangements, including remote work and the gig economy, brings with it a host of legal and ethical considerations that both employers and employees must navigate. These considerations are essential for ensuring fair treatment, compliance with laws, and the creation of a healthy and sustainable work environment.

One of the primary legal considerations is the classification of workers. Misclassifying employees as independent contractors can lead to significant legal repercussions. Employees are entitled to certain benefits and protections under labor laws, such as minimum wage, overtime pay, health benefits, and workers' compensation. Independent contractors, on the other hand, do not receive these benefits, but they have more control over how they perform their work. Companies must carefully determine the correct classification of their workers to avoid legal disputes and potential penalties.

Labor laws and regulations vary significantly across regions and countries, making compliance a complex issue for companies with a geographically dispersed workforce. Employers must ensure that they adhere to the labor laws applicable in each location where their employees work. This includes understanding and complying with regulations related to working hours, overtime, health and safety standards, and termination policies. Failure to comply with local labor laws can result in legal action, fines, and damage to the company's reputation.

Data privacy and cybersecurity are critical legal and ethical concerns in flexible work environments. With employees accessing company systems and data from various locations and devices, the risk of data breaches and cyberattacks increases. Employers must implement robust cybersecurity measures, such as encryption, secure access protocols, and regular security audits, to protect sensitive information. Additionally, companies should provide training to employees on best practices for maintaining data security and protecting personal information.

Health and safety regulations are also relevant in the context of remote work. Employers have a legal and ethical obligation to ensure that their employees' work environments are safe, even when they are working from home. This may involve providing ergonomic assessments, resources for mental health support, and guidelines for maintaining a healthy work-life balance. Ensuring employees have access to necessary equipment and a safe workspace is part of this responsibility.

The ethical considerations in flexible work extend beyond legal compliance to include fairness and equity. Employers must ensure that all employees, regardless of their work arrangement, have equal access to opportunities for career advancement, professional development, and recognition. This includes providing remote workers with the same training, mentorship, and promotion opportunities as their on-site counterparts. Addressing unconscious bias and ensuring that performance evaluations are based on merit and outcomes, rather than physical presence, are crucial for fostering an inclusive work culture.

Transparency and clear communication are fundamental ethical practices in managing a flexible workforce. Employers should clearly communicate expectations, policies, and procedures related to remote work and flexible arrangements. This includes outlining performance metrics, availability requirements, and communication protocols. Regular check-ins and feedback sessions can help maintain alignment and address any issues promptly.

Work-life balance is another important ethical consideration. While flexible work arrangements can enhance work-life balance by providing greater control over work schedules, they can also lead to overwork and burnout if not managed properly. Employers should encourage employees to set boundaries, take regular breaks, and prioritize their well-being. Providing resources such as mental health support and promoting a culture that values balance can help mitigate these risks.

The environmental impact of flexible work is an emerging ethical consideration. Remote work can reduce carbon footprints by decreasing the need for commuting and office space. However, it also shifts energy consumption to employees' homes. Companies can support sustainability by encouraging energy-efficient practices and considering the environmental impact of their remote work policies.

Chapter 5: Embracing Technological Disruption

Technological disruption is reshaping industries and redefining job roles at an unprecedented pace. At the forefront of this transformation is artificial intelligence (AI), which is not only revolutionizing how businesses operate but also creating new opportunities and challenges for the workforce. Embracing technological disruption requires an understanding of AI's impact on various sectors, the emergence of new job roles, and the cultivation of a mindset that values growth and adaptability. This chapter explores these themes and provides insights into how individuals and organizations can prepare for and thrive amidst these profound changes.

AI's impact on industries is both far-reaching and transformative. In healthcare, AI-driven diagnostics and personalized treatment plans are enhancing patient care and efficiency. In finance, algorithms for predictive analytics and automated trading are revolutionizing how investments are managed, and decisions are made. The retail industry is leveraging AI for personalized customer experiences, inventory management, and supply chain optimization. Manufacturing is being reshaped by AI through advanced robotics, predictive maintenance, and smart production processes. These examples illustrate just a few of the ways AI is transforming industries, leading to increased productivity, innovation, and new business models.

With these advancements come emerging job roles and new career paths. As traditional tasks become automated, there is a growing demand for roles that focus on developing, managing, and optimizing AI systems. Data scientists, machine learning engineers, AI ethicists, and automation specialists are among the new professions gaining prominence. Additionally, roles that emphasize human-AI collaboration, such as AI trainers and explainability experts, are becoming essential. These new career paths require a blend of technical expertise, creativity, and ethical considerations, highlighting the need for continuous learning and skill development.

Making sure to cultivate a growth mindset and adaptability is crucial in the face of technological disruption. A growth mindset, characterized by the belief that abilities and intelligence can be developed through effort and learning, enables individuals to embrace challenges and view failures as opportunities for growth. This mindset fosters resilience and a proactive approach to personal and professional development. Adaptability, the ability to adjust to new conditions and embrace change, is equally important. As technology evolves, being open to learning new skills and pivoting to new roles becomes essential for maintaining relevance and success in the workforce.

We can prepare for industry-specific technological changes by staying informed about the latest advancements and understanding their implications for one's field. Professionals must actively seek out training and educational opportunities to keep their skills current. This may involve enrolling in courses, attending workshops and conferences, or participating in industry forums and online communities. Organizations also play a critical role by providing resources and support for employee development, fostering a culture of continuous learning, and encouraging innovation.

In order to mitigate risks associated with technological disruption requires a thoughtful and strategic approach. While AI and automation offer significant benefits, they also pose challenges such as job displacement, data privacy concerns, and ethical dilemmas. Addressing these risks involves developing policies and practices that ensure fair treatment of workers, protecting sensitive information, and promoting ethical AI use. Companies must balance the pursuit of technological advancements with considerations for social impact, ensuring that innovation benefits society as a whole.

Technological disruption is about more than just keeping up with the latest technologies; it involves understanding AI's transformative impact on industries, preparing for new job roles, cultivating a growth mindset, staying adaptable, and mitigating associated risks. By adopting these strategies, individuals and organizations can navigate the complexities of technological change and harness its potential to drive innovation and progress. This chapter delves into these aspects, offering guidance on how to thrive in an era of rapid technological advancement and disruption.

AI's impact on various industries and job roles is profound and far-reaching, promising both opportunities and challenges as it reshapes the landscape of work and business operations. In healthcare, AI is revolutionizing diagnostics and treatment. Advanced algorithms can analyze medical images and patient data with remarkable accuracy, often surpassing human capabilities in detecting diseases like cancer at early stages. AI-driven predictive analytics help in identifying at-risk patients, enabling preventative care and personalized treatment plans. The automation of administrative tasks allows healthcare professionals to focus more on patient care, improving overall efficiency and outcomes.

In the finance sector, AI is transforming how we manage money and make financial decisions. Robo-advisors use AI to provide personalized investment advice based on individual financial goals and risk tolerance, making sophisticated financial planning accessible to a broader audience. Fraud detection systems powered by AI can analyze transaction patterns in real time, identifying suspicious activities and reducing financial crime. AI also enhances trading strategies, with algorithms capable of analyzing vast amounts of data to predict market trends and execute trades at optimal times, thus increasing profitability.

The retail industry is experiencing a significant transformation driven by AI. Personalized shopping experiences are now the norm, with AI analyzing customer data to recommend products tailored to individual preferences. Inventory management systems powered by AI predict demand with high accuracy, ensuring that shelves are stocked with the right products while minimizing waste. Customer service is also being revolutionized by AI chatbots, which handle a significant portion of customer inquiries, providing quick and efficient support around the clock.

Manufacturing is undergoing a renaissance thanks to AI and automation. Smart factories utilize AI to monitor and optimize production processes in real time, enhancing efficiency and reducing downtime. Predictive maintenance, driven by AI, foresees equipment failures before they occur, allowing for timely interventions and minimizing disruptions. Robots powered by AI perform complex tasks with precision, increasing production capabilities and safety in environments that are hazardous for human workers.

The transportation industry is on the cusp of transformation with the advent of AI. Self-driving cars and trucks, equipped with advanced AI systems, promise to revolutionize logistics and commuting by reducing accidents caused by human error and optimizing fuel efficiency. AI in traffic management systems can predict and alleviate congestion, improving urban mobility. Ride-sharing platforms leverage AI to match riders with drivers efficiently, reducing wait times and costs.

Education is another sector where AI is making a significant impact. Personalized learning platforms adapt to individual student's learning styles and paces, providing customized educational experiences. AI can identify areas where students struggle and suggest resources to help them improve. Administrative tasks such as grading and scheduling are streamlined with AI, freeing educators to focus more on teaching and student engagement.

In agriculture, AI is enhancing productivity and sustainability. AI-driven analytics optimize crop planning, pest control, and irrigation, ensuring better yields and resource management. Drones and autonomous machinery, powered by AI, perform labor-intensive tasks like planting and harvesting with greater efficiency and precision, reducing labor costs and environmental impact.

The impact of AI on job roles is equally transformative. As AI automates routine and repetitive tasks, the demand for human labor in these areas decreases, while the need for roles that involve complex decision-making, creativity, and emotional intelligence increases. Data scientists and machine learning engineers are in high demand, as they are essential for developing and implementing AI systems. AI trainers and ethicists are emerging roles focused on ensuring that AI systems operate correctly and ethically.

Roles that involve human-AI collaboration are becoming more prevalent. For instance, in healthcare, AI assists doctors in diagnostics, but the human touch is irreplaceable in patient care and decision-making. In creative industries, AI can generate ideas and content, but human creativity and judgment remain crucial for refining and finalizing those outputs. Emotional intelligence and interpersonal skills are increasingly valued as automation takes over technical tasks, highlighting the importance of human-centric roles such as counseling, leadership, and customer service.

The emerging roles are characterized by their focus on leveraging technology to solve complex problems, enhance productivity, and drive innovation across various sectors. Here are some of the key emerging job roles and new career paths in the AI-driven landscape:

Data scientists are at the forefront of the AI revolution. They are responsible for collecting, analyzing, and interpreting large volumes of data to extract meaningful insights that can drive business decisions. Data scientists use statistical methods, machine learning algorithms, and data visualization techniques to identify patterns and trends in data, helping organizations understand their customers, optimize operations, and predict future outcomes.

Machine learning engineers specialize in designing, building, and deploying machine learning models. They work closely with data scientists to develop algorithms that can learn from data and make predictions or decisions without explicit programming. Machine learning engineers need strong programming skills, expertise in algorithms and data structures, and an understanding of various machine learning frameworks and tools. Their work is essential in fields such as natural language processing, computer vision, and recommendation systems.

AI ethicists play a crucial role in ensuring that AI systems are developed and used responsibly. They address the ethical implications of AI, such as bias, privacy, and transparency. AI ethicists work with engineers, policymakers, and business leaders to develop guidelines and frameworks that ensure AI technologies are fair, accountable, and aligned with societal values. Their work helps mitigate the risks associated with AI and fosters public trust in these technologies.

Automation specialists focus on identifying opportunities for automation within organizations and implementing solutions to streamline processes. They use tools like robotic process automation (RPA) to automate repetitive tasks, freeing up human workers for more strategic and creative activities. Automation specialists need to understand both the technical aspects of automation technologies and the business processes they are designed to improve.

AI trainers are responsible for teaching AI systems how to perform specific tasks. This often involves curating and annotating large datasets that the AI can use to learn and improve its performance. AI trainers play a critical role in areas such as natural language processing, where they might train a chatbot to understand and respond to customer queries accurately. Their work ensures that AI systems are well-trained and capable of delivering reliable results.

Explainability experts focus on making AI systems transparent and understandable to non-technical stakeholders. They develop methods and tools to interpret the decision-making processes of AI models, ensuring that users can understand why a model made a particular decision. This is especially important in regulated industries like finance and healthcare, where understanding the rationale behind AI decisions is crucial for compliance and trust.

In addition to these technical roles, there is a growing demand for professionals who can bridge the gap between AI and business. AI project managers oversee AI initiatives within organizations, ensuring that projects are delivered on time, within budget, and aligned with business objectives. They coordinate cross-functional teams, manage resources, and communicate progress to stakeholders, playing a pivotal role in the successful implementation of AI projects.

Digital transformation consultants help organizations navigate the complexities of adopting new technologies. They assess an organization's current capabilities, identify areas for improvement, and develop strategies for integrating AI and other advanced technologies into existing workflows. Digital transformation consultants need a deep understanding of technology and strong business acumen to guide organizations through their digital journeys.

The creative industries are also seeing new roles emerge as AI becomes more integrated into content creation. AI content creators and curators use AI tools to generate and refine creative works, such as music, art, writing, and design. While AI can assist in producing content, human creativity and judgment are essential for ensuring quality and originality. These roles require a blend of artistic skills and technical proficiency with AI tools.

Cybersecurity analysts are increasingly important in the AI era, as the integration of advanced technologies introduces new vulnerabilities and threats. These professionals use AI-driven tools to detect, analyze, and respond to cyber threats in real-time. They also develop strategies to protect sensitive data and ensure the security of AI systems, making their role crucial for safeguarding organizational assets.

Cultivating a growth mindset and adaptability is crucial in today's rapidly changing world, where technological advancements and evolving market demands require continuous learning and flexibility. A growth mindset, as defined by psychologist Carol Dweck, involves the belief that abilities and intelligence can develop through dedication, hard work, and learning. This mindset contrasts with a fixed mindset, which assumes that talents and abilities remain static and unchangeable. Embracing a growth mindset and enhancing adaptability are vital for personal and professional success in the face of constant change.

To cultivate a growth mindset, begin by viewing challenges as opportunities for growth rather than obstacles to avoid. Challenges push individuals out of their comfort zones and stimulate personal and professional development. When difficulties arise, see them as chances to learn new skills and gain valuable experiences. By reframing challenges in this way, you reduce fear of failure and increase your willingness to take risks.

Learning from feedback is another crucial aspect of developing a growth mindset. Constructive criticism provides insights into areas for improvement and helps identify specific actions to enhance performance. Instead of perceiving feedback as a personal attack, treat it as valuable information that can guide your development. Actively seek feedback from mentors, peers, and supervisors, and use it to refine your skills and approaches.

Setting goals that are both challenging and achievable is key to fostering a growth mindset. Establish clear, specific objectives that push you to expand your capabilities. Break these goals into smaller, manageable steps to make progress more tangible and to maintain motivation. Celebrate small victories along the way to acknowledge your efforts and sustain momentum.

Adopting a lifelong learning attitude is essential for cultivating a growth mindset. Stay curious and open to new knowledge and experiences. Engage in continuous education through formal courses, workshops, online learning platforms, and self-study. Explore diverse subjects and disciplines to broaden your perspective and enhance your ability to connect ideas across different fields.

Surrounding yourself with a supportive and growth-oriented community significantly impacts your mindset. Engage with individuals who share a commitment to growth and learning. Participate in professional networks, join study groups, and seek out mentors who provide guidance and encouragement. Being part of a community that values development reinforces your own commitment to a growth mindset.

Adaptability involves the ability to adjust to new conditions and navigate change effectively. To enhance adaptability, start by building resilience. Resilience encompasses the capacity to recover quickly from setbacks and maintain focus on long-term goals. Build resilience by developing coping strategies for stress, maintaining a positive outlook, and managing uncertainty.

Embrace flexibility in your thinking and approaches. Be open to new ideas, perspectives, and methods. Avoid becoming too attached to a single way of doing things, and experiment with different approaches. Flexibility allows you to pivot when circumstances change and find innovative solutions to emerging challenges.

Develop strong problem-solving skills as another component of adaptability. Enhance your ability to analyze situations, identify key issues, and develop creative solutions. Practice thinking critically and systematically, breaking down complex problems into manageable parts. This approach helps you respond effectively to unexpected challenges and adapt your strategies as needed.

Stay informed about industry trends and technological advancements to increase adaptability. Keep up-to-date with changes in your field by reading industry publications, attending conferences, and participating in professional development opportunities. Understanding the broader context in which you work enables you to anticipate changes and prepare proactively.

Build a diverse skill set to handle a variety of tasks and roles. Develop both technical and soft skills to increase your versatility. For example, combine expertise in specific technologies with strong communication and teamwork abilities. A diverse skill set enables you to transition smoothly between different projects and roles, making you more resilient to change.

Navigating industry-specific technological changes requires more than a checklist; it demands a strategic and adaptive approach that blends foresight with actionable insights. As sectors like healthcare, finance, manufacturing, and education undergo transformative innovations, professionals and organizations must seamlessly integrate these advancements to not only remain competitive but to excel.

Understanding the pulse of technological trends is paramount. It's not merely about staying abreast of the latest innovations but deeply immersing in the implications these advancements hold for the industry. For instance, AI is revolutionizing diagnostics in healthcare, driving predictive analytics and automated trading in finance, and enhancing precision and efficiency in manufacturing. Recognizing these shifts is the initial step in preparing for future challenges and opportunities.

Continuous learning is critical. Engaging in specialized courses and training programs equips professionals with the expertise needed to handle new technologies and methodologies. For example, a finance professional might delve into blockchain technology, while a manufacturing expert could focus on mastering advanced robotics. This commitment to education builds a bridge to future opportunities, ensuring that skills remain sharp and relevant.

Flexibility and openness are essential. Technological advancements often necessitate changes in how tasks are performed and processes are managed. Embracing new tools and practices with a willingness to adapt fosters a culture of innovation and continuous improvement within the organization.

Collaboration with industry peers and experts is invaluable. Joining professional associations, participating in online forums, and attending networking events facilitate the exchange of knowledge and best practices. This collaborative learning environment enhances understanding and provides diverse perspectives on tackling technological changes.

Strategic planning is crucial for navigating technological advancements. Regular assessments of current capabilities and identification of areas where new technologies could enhance efficiency and productivity are essential. Developing a roadmap for integrating these technologies ensures a smooth transition and minimizes disruptions.

Investing in the right tools and infrastructure supports technological advancements. Upgrading hardware, software, and networks is necessary for leveraging new technologies effectively. Ensuring that the organization has the technical capacity to adopt and utilize the latest innovations positions it for future success.

Prioritizing cybersecurity measures is vital. As new technologies emerge, so do new security threats. Implementing robust cybersecurity protocols, conducting regular security audits, and providing employee training on best practices for data protection are essential for safeguarding the organization's assets.

Fostering a culture of continuous improvement and innovation within the organization is imperative. Encouraging employees to experiment with new technologies and propose creative solutions cultivates an environment where adaptability thrives. Recognizing and rewarding efforts to innovate reinforces the value of adaptability and forward-thinking.

Monitoring the impact of technological changes and adjusting strategies accordingly ensures agility. Staying vigilant for emerging trends and market shifts that could influence operations is crucial. Being prepared to pivot and refine approaches based on new information and insights maintains competitiveness and responsiveness.

Companies must adopt a proactive and strategic approach to prepare for and mitigate risks associated with technological disruption. This involves understanding potential threats, implementing robust risk management strategies, and fostering a culture of resilience and adaptability within the organization.

Firstly, companies should conduct a comprehensive risk assessment to identify potential vulnerabilities and areas of disruption. This involves analyzing the impact of new technologies on existing business processes, market position, and competitive landscape. By understanding these risks, companies can develop targeted strategies to address them.

Investing in continuous education and training is essential. As new technologies emerge, employees must be equipped with the necessary skills to utilize them effectively. Regular training programs, workshops, and certifications help ensure that the workforce remains competent and capable of handling technological changes. This investment in human capital not only mitigates the risk of skills obsolescence but also fosters a culture of continuous improvement and innovation.

Implementing robust cybersecurity measures is critical in mitigating the risks associated with technological disruption. As companies adopt new technologies, they must ensure that their data and systems are protected against cyber threats. This includes employing advanced security protocols, conducting regular security audits, and providing employees with training on cybersecurity best practices. Ensuring robust data privacy and protection measures will help safeguard sensitive information and maintain stakeholder trust.

Developing a flexible and scalable IT infrastructure is another key strategy. Companies should invest in technologies and systems that can adapt to changing business needs and technological advancements. Cloud computing, for example, offers scalable solutions that can grow with the business and provide the flexibility needed to integrate new technologies seamlessly. A resilient IT infrastructure minimizes downtime and ensures business continuity during periods of technological change.

Strategic partnerships and collaborations can also play a vital role in mitigating risks. By partnering with technology providers, industry experts, and other businesses, companies can gain access to cutting-edge technologies and insights that help navigate the complexities of technological disruption. These collaborations can provide valuable support, share best practices, and offer innovative solutions that enhance the company's capabilities and competitiveness.

Companies should establish a robust change management framework to manage the transition to new technologies effectively. This involves clear communication of the change vision, engaging stakeholders at all levels, and providing the necessary resources and support to facilitate the transition. Effective change management minimizes resistance, enhances buy-in, and ensures a smoother implementation of new technologies.

Regular monitoring and evaluation of technological advancements are essential to stay ahead of potential disruptions. Companies should establish a system for continuous monitoring of industry trends, emerging technologies, and market dynamics. This proactive approach allows companies to anticipate changes, adapt strategies, and make informed decisions that align with technological advancements.

Building a culture of innovation and agility is crucial for long-term success. Companies should encourage experimentation, reward innovative thinking, and create an environment where employees feel empowered to explore new ideas and approaches. This culture of innovation fosters resilience and adaptability, enabling the company to respond swiftly to technological disruptions and seize new opportunities.

Lastly, diversification of products, services, and markets can help mitigate risks associated with technological disruption. By diversifying their portfolio, companies can reduce dependency on a single technology or market, spreading the risk across different areas. This strategic diversification enhances stability and provides a buffer against the impact of disruptive technologies.

Chapter 6: Collaboration and Soft Skills

As artificial intelligence and other advanced technologies continue to integrate into various aspects of business operations, the ability to effectively collaborate with both human and AI counterparts becomes a critical determinant of success. While technical proficiency remains essential, it is the complementary soft skills that often differentiate individuals and teams in achieving high performance and innovation.

Human-AI collaboration is a cornerstone of this new era. AI systems excel at processing vast amounts of data, identifying patterns, and performing repetitive tasks with precision. However, they lack the nuanced understanding, creativity, and ethical judgment that humans bring to the table. Effective collaboration between humans and AI not only enhances productivity but also drives innovative solutions that neither could achieve alone. This synergy underscores the need for strong communication and interpersonal skills, as clear and effective interaction is fundamental to maximizing the potential of human-AI partnerships.

Emotional intelligence and empathy are equally crucial in this context. These skills enable individuals to navigate the complexities of human relationships, fostering a positive and inclusive workplace culture. In environments where teams are increasingly diverse and globally distributed, understanding and managing emotions—both one's own and those of others—enhances team cohesion and performance. Emotional intelligence supports better conflict resolution, improves leadership effectiveness, and drives overall job satisfaction and engagement.

The dynamics of teamwork are also evolving in AI-augmented workplaces. As AI handles more technical and routine tasks, human teams are freed to focus on strategic, creative, and relational aspects of work. This shift requires a reevaluation of teamwork strategies to ensure that human contributions are optimized and that collaboration remains seamless. Effective teamwork in this new landscape leverages collaborative tools and technologies, promotes inclusivity, and balances individual and collective efforts.

Conflict resolution and negotiation skills remain as relevant as ever, if not more so. With the complexity of interactions in a technologically advanced workplace, conflicts can arise from various sources, including misunderstandings, misaligned expectations, and resistance to change. Developing skills to address and resolve these conflicts constructively ensures a harmonious work environment and facilitates smooth transitions during technological integration. Similarly, negotiation skills are essential in reaching agreements that are beneficial for all parties involved, whether in internal team settings or external stakeholder interactions.

As we delve into this chapter, we will explore the critical role of soft skills in enhancing human-AI collaboration, the importance of communication and interpersonal skills, the development of emotional intelligence and empathy, the dynamics of teamwork in an AI-augmented workplace, and effective strategies for conflict resolution and negotiation. By mastering these skills, individuals and organizations can navigate the complexities of the modern workplace, harnessing the full potential of both human and technological capabilities to drive sustained success and innovation.

In the landscape of modern business, integrating AI with human capabilities is not just advantageous but essential. As AI technologies evolve, they offer unprecedented efficiencies and capabilities, yet their potential is fully realized only when they complement and enhance human abilities. This symbiotic relationship between human intelligence and artificial intelligence can transform industries, drive innovation, and significantly boost productivity.

The necessity of integrating AI with human capabilities becomes evident when considering the unique strengths each brings to the table. AI excels at processing large volumes of data, recognizing patterns, and performing repetitive tasks with speed and accuracy that far surpass human abilities. However, AI lacks the nuanced understanding, contextual awareness, and ethical judgment inherent to human intelligence. Humans provide the creativity, critical thinking, and ethical considerations that guide AI applications towards meaningful and responsible use.

Numerous case studies highlight the successful integration of AI and human collaboration across various industries. In healthcare, for instance, AI systems assist radiologists by rapidly analyzing medical images and identifying potential anomalies. While AI can process and flag these images quickly, the radiologist provides the necessary context, clinical expertise, and final judgment, ensuring accurate diagnoses and personalized patient care. This collaboration enhances diagnostic accuracy and allows healthcare professionals to focus on complex cases requiring deeper clinical insight.

In the finance sector, AI-driven algorithms analyze market data to identify trends and predict investment opportunities. Financial analysts and portfolio managers then use these insights to make informed decisions, considering factors beyond the scope of AI, such as market sentiment and geopolitical events. This partnership between AI and human expertise leads to more robust investment strategies and improved financial performance.

The retail industry also showcases the benefits of human-AI collaboration. AI systems analyze customer data to personalize shopping experiences, recommend products, and manage inventory efficiently. Retail professionals leverage these insights to design targeted marketing campaigns, curate product selections, and enhance customer service. The result is a seamless shopping experience that meets customer needs more effectively and drives sales.

Humans play a crucial role in providing context, creativity, and ethical judgment to AI systems. Contextual understanding allows humans to interpret AI-generated insights within the broader framework of their business environment. Creativity enables the generation of innovative ideas and solutions that AI alone cannot conceive. Ethical judgment ensures that AI applications adhere to moral and societal standards, preventing misuse and fostering trust.

The benefits of human-AI collaboration extend beyond specific industry applications. Increased productivity is a direct outcome, as AI automates routine tasks, allowing human workers to focus on higher-value activities. Innovation flourishes when humans and AI combine their strengths to tackle complex problems and develop novel solutions. Efficiency improves as AI optimizes processes and humans enhance these optimizations with strategic insights and adaptability.

Human-AI collaboration fosters a culture of continuous learning and improvement. As humans interact with AI systems, they gain new skills and knowledge, staying abreast of technological advancements. This continuous adaptation ensures that both the workforce and the organization remain competitive in an ever-changing market.

Effective communication is the cornerstone of successful collaboration and teamwork, especially in a diverse, AI-augmented workforce. As AI takes on more roles within organizations, the human ability to communicate clearly and effectively becomes even more critical. Enhancing communication and interpersonal skills ensures that teams can work together harmoniously, leveraging both human and AI capabilities to achieve their goals.

The role of effective communication in fostering collaboration and teamwork cannot be overstated. Clear communication helps align team members with shared goals, clarifies expectations, and facilitates the efficient exchange of ideas. In an environment where AI systems provide data-driven insights and automation, human team members must communicate these findings and their implications effectively to ensure that everyone understands and can act on the information. Miscommunication can lead to errors, misunderstandings, and missed opportunities, undermining the potential benefits of human-AI collaboration.

Improving verbal and written communication involves several key techniques. For verbal communication, focus on clarity and conciseness. Articulate your thoughts clearly and avoid jargon or overly complex language that can confuse listeners. Tailoring your message to your audience is crucial; consider their level of expertise and perspective when conveying information. For written communication, structure your messages logically, use bullet points for clarity, and employ visual aids like charts or graphs to support your points. Reviewing and editing written content for coherence and accuracy can also significantly enhance its effectiveness.

Active listening and constructive feedback are vital components of effective communication. Active listening involves fully concentrating on the speaker, understanding their message, and responding thoughtfully. This practice helps build trust and ensures that all team members feel heard and valued. Constructive feedback, delivered with respect and empathy, fosters a culture of continuous improvement and learning. Providing specific, actionable feedback helps colleagues understand their strengths and areas for development, promoting personal and professional growth.

Building relationships and trust in a diverse, AI-augmented workforce is essential for effective collaboration. Trust is the foundation of any successful team, enabling open communication, risk-taking, and innovation. To build trust, demonstrate reliability, competence, and integrity in your interactions. Engage in regular check-ins with team members, showing genuine interest in their work and well-being. Celebrating successes and recognizing individual contributions also strengthens team cohesion and morale.

In a diverse workforce, cultural awareness and sensitivity are critical. Understanding and respecting different cultural norms, communication styles, and perspectives can prevent misunderstandings and foster a more inclusive environment. Encourage team members to share their backgrounds and experiences, enriching the team's collective knowledge and promoting a culture of respect and inclusion.

Tools and technologies that facilitate communication in remote and hybrid work environments are indispensable in today's workplace. Platforms like Slack, Microsoft Teams, and Zoom enable real-time communication and collaboration, bridging the gap between remote and in-office workers. These tools offer features like instant messaging, video conferencing, file sharing, and collaborative document editing, making it easier for teams to stay connected and productive regardless of their physical location.

Effective use of these tools involves more than just familiarity with their functionalities. Establishing clear communication protocols and best practices is crucial. For example, determine the appropriate channels for different types of communication, such as using email for formal announcements and instant messaging for quick queries. Encourage regular video meetings to maintain face-to-face interaction, which is vital for building relationships and trust. Additionally, leveraging collaborative platforms like Google Workspace or Microsoft 365 can streamline workflows and enhance team collaboration on projects.

Emotional intelligence (EI) is a crucial attribute in the modern workplace, particularly in environments augmented by AI and advanced technologies. It encompasses the ability to recognize, understand, and manage our own emotions, as well as the ability to recognize, understand, and influence the emotions of others. Emotional intelligence is composed of five key components: self-awareness, self-regulation, motivation, empathy, and social skills.

Self-awareness involves recognizing and understanding one's own emotions. It allows individuals to assess their strengths and weaknesses accurately, leading to better decision-making and more effective personal and professional interactions. Self-regulation refers to the ability to manage and control one's emotional responses. This skill helps individuals stay composed, think clearly, and respond constructively to challenging situations. Motivation is the drive to achieve goals for personal fulfillment rather than external rewards. It fuels persistence, resilience, and a positive attitude, even in the face of setbacks. Empathy involves understanding and sharing the feelings of others, which is crucial for building strong interpersonal relationships and fostering a supportive workplace. Social skills encompass the ability to communicate effectively, manage relationships, and navigate social complexities, all of which are essential for teamwork and leadership.

Emotional intelligence significantly enhances leadership, team dynamics, and workplace culture. Leaders with high emotional intelligence can inspire and motivate their teams, navigate conflicts with ease, and create an environment where employees feel valued and understood. These leaders are adept at reading the emotional currents within their teams and can adjust their approach to suit the needs of their employees. This adaptability fosters trust and loyalty, leading to higher levels of engagement and productivity. In team dynamics, emotional intelligence facilitates better communication, collaboration, and conflict resolution. Teams with emotionally intelligent members are more cohesive, adaptable, and effective in achieving their goals. Moreover, a workplace culture that values and promotes emotional intelligence is typically more inclusive, innovative, and resilient.

Developing empathy is a cornerstone of emotional intelligence. One effective strategy for cultivating empathy is perspective-taking, which involves putting oneself in another person's shoes to understand their thoughts, feelings, and experiences. This practice can enhance interpersonal relationships by fostering greater understanding and reducing biases. Active listening is another crucial strategy. It requires fully concentrating on the speaker, understanding their message, responding thoughtfully, and remembering what was said. Active listening demonstrates respect and validation, making others feel heard and valued.

The impact of emotional intelligence extends to conflict resolution, stress management, and employee engagement. In conflict resolution, emotionally intelligent individuals can navigate disputes with a calm and constructive approach, addressing the underlying emotions and finding mutually beneficial solutions. They can de-escalate tense situations and promote harmony within the team. For stress management, self-regulation and self-awareness enable individuals to recognize stress triggers and implement strategies to manage their reactions. This leads to better mental health and well-being. Higher emotional intelligence also correlates with greater employee engagement. Employees who feel understood and supported by their leaders and peers are more likely to be committed, motivated, and productive.

Real-world examples of emotional intelligence in action illustrate its profound impact. Consider a healthcare leader who uses empathy and active listening to understand the concerns of their team during a high-stress period. By addressing these concerns and providing support, the leader fosters a more resilient and cohesive team. Another example is a project manager in a tech company who leverages social skills and motivation to inspire a team working on a challenging project. The manager's ability to navigate the team's emotions and maintain a positive atmosphere results in a successful project delivery and high team morale.

The integration of AI technologies is reshaping the nature of teamwork, bringing both challenges and opportunities. As AI takes on more roles within organizations, the way teams operate and collaborate is evolving. This transformation requires a rethinking of traditional teamwork dynamics to ensure that both human and AI contributions are optimized for maximum effectiveness.

The evolving nature of teamwork with AI integration involves a shift in how tasks are assigned and executed. AI can handle repetitive, data-intensive tasks with speed and accuracy, freeing human team members to focus on strategic, creative, and complex problem-solving activities. This division of labor requires clear communication and coordination to ensure seamless collaboration between human and AI agents. Human team members must understand how to interpret and act on AI-generated insights, while AI systems need to be trained and fine-tuned based on human feedback.

Diverse teams are crucial in leveraging AI for innovation. A mix of skills, perspectives, and experiences enables teams to approach problems more holistically and creatively. Diversity enhances the ability to develop AI solutions that are inclusive and equitable, reducing the risk of biases that can arise from homogenous groups. By bringing together individuals from different backgrounds, teams can better identify and mitigate potential biases in AI algorithms and applications. Moreover, diverse teams are more adept at brainstorming innovative uses for AI, driving both technological and business advancements.

Collaborative tools and platforms play a vital role in enhancing teamwork and project management in an AI-augmented workplace. Tools like Slack, Microsoft Teams, and Zoom facilitate real-time communication and collaboration, allowing team members to share information, discuss ideas, and resolve issues quickly. Project management platforms such as Trello, Asana, and Monday.com provide structured environments for tracking progress, assigning tasks, and managing deadlines. These tools often integrate AI features that can automate administrative tasks, provide project insights, and predict potential bottlenecks, further enhancing efficiency and productivity.

Managing remote and hybrid teams effectively is essential as these work models become more prevalent. Best practices for managing such teams include establishing clear communication protocols, setting regular check-ins and virtual meetings, and fostering a sense of inclusion and engagement among remote workers.

Leaders should ensure that remote team members have access to the same information and opportunities as their on-site counterparts. Encouraging collaboration through virtual team-building activities and providing support for remote work challenges can help maintain team cohesion and morale.

Balancing individual contributions and collective efforts in AI-enhanced projects is another key aspect of teamwork. Each team member brings unique strengths and expertise that contribute to the overall success of the project. Clearly defining roles and responsibilities helps ensure that everyone understands their part in the larger effort. Encouraging collaboration and knowledge sharing allows team members to learn from each other and leverage each other's strengths. AI systems can facilitate this by providing data-driven insights and automating routine tasks, enabling human team members to focus on high-impact activities.

In an AI-augmented workplace, it is important to create an environment where both human and AI contributions are valued and integrated seamlessly. This involves ongoing training and development to keep team members up-to-date with AI advancements and best practices. Providing opportunities for professional growth and encouraging continuous learning helps ensure that team members remain engaged and capable of leveraging AI effectively.

For instance, a marketing team using AI to analyze customer data and predict trends can focus on crafting personalized marketing strategies and creative campaigns based on AI insights. The AI system handles data crunching and pattern recognition, while the human team members bring creativity, strategic thinking, and emotional intelligence to the table. This collaboration results in more effective marketing efforts and a better customer experience.

In any workplace, conflicts are inevitable due to diverse perspectives, varying interests, and the complexities of team dynamics. Understanding the sources of conflict and developing effective resolution and negotiation skills are essential for maintaining a productive and harmonious work environment. This is especially true in AI-augmented environments where the integration of advanced technologies introduces new dimensions of collaboration and potential friction.

Understanding the sources of conflict in the workplace involves recognizing that conflicts can arise from multiple factors. Common sources include miscommunication, differences in values or priorities, competition for resources, and personality clashes. In AI-augmented workplaces, additional sources of conflict may stem from resistance to technological changes, concerns about job security, and misunderstandings about the role and capabilities of AI systems. By identifying these underlying issues, managers and team members can address them proactively and prevent escalation.

Techniques for resolving conflicts constructively involve mediation, collaborative problem-solving, and fostering open communication. Mediation involves a neutral third party who facilitates a dialogue between conflicting parties to help them reach a mutually acceptable solution. This technique is effective in diffusing tension and encouraging cooperative behavior. Collaborative problem-solving, on the other hand, focuses on finding a solution that satisfies the needs of all parties involved. This approach encourages team members to work together to identify the root cause of the conflict and develop creative solutions. Open communication is essential throughout this process, as it ensures that all parties feel heard and valued, reducing the likelihood of future conflicts.

Negotiation skills play a crucial role in reaching mutually beneficial agreements. Effective negotiation involves understanding the interests and goals of both parties, exploring options for mutual gain, and finding common ground. In AI-augmented environments, negotiations might involve decisions about the allocation of tasks between humans and AI, the implementation of new technologies, or the distribution of resources. Successful negotiators use active listening, empathy, and strategic thinking to create win-win scenarios that address the concerns of all stakeholders.

Strategies for preparing for and conducting effective negotiations include thorough preparation, setting clear objectives, and maintaining flexibility. Preparation involves researching the issues at hand, understanding the interests and positions of all parties, and anticipating potential challenges. Setting clear objectives ensures that negotiators have a clear understanding of what they want to achieve and can communicate their goals effectively. Maintaining flexibility allows negotiators to adapt their strategies based on new information and evolving dynamics during the negotiation process. Building rapport and trust with the other party is also crucial, as it facilitates open dialogue and increases the likelihood of reaching a satisfactory agreement.

Case studies of successful conflict resolution and negotiation in AI-augmented environments highlight the importance of these skills. For instance, in a technology company implementing AI-driven customer service solutions, conflict arose between the customer service team and the IT department. The customer service team feared job losses and felt excluded from the decision-making process. Mediation sessions facilitated by a neutral third party helped both teams express their concerns and expectations. Collaborative problem-solving workshops were conducted to identify ways in which AI could enhance, rather than replace, the roles of customer service representatives. As a result, a new hybrid model was developed where AI handled routine inquiries, allowing human agents to focus on complex customer issues, thereby improving job satisfaction and customer experience.

In another example, a manufacturing firm faced internal conflict over the adoption of AI-powered predictive maintenance systems. The operations team resisted the change, fearing disruptions to established processes. Through a series of negotiation meetings, facilitated by a skilled mediator, both sides were able to express their concerns and explore the benefits of the new system. The negotiations resulted in a phased implementation plan that included training sessions for the operations team, ensuring they felt prepared and supported during the transition. This approach minimized resistance and fostered a collaborative spirit, ultimately leading to a successful integration of the new technology.

In an era where AI and advanced technologies are becoming integral to business operations, the critical role of soft skills in enhancing human-AI collaboration cannot be overstated. Throughout this chapter, we have explored the profound impact that effective communication, emotional intelligence, teamwork, and conflict resolution skills have on creating a productive and harmonious workplace. These skills are essential not only for leveraging AI technologies effectively but also for fostering a work environment where human capabilities are fully realized and valued.

Developing strong communication skills is paramount in this context. Effective verbal and written communication, active listening, and providing constructive feedback ensure that team members are aligned and can collaborate seamlessly. Building relationships and trust in a diverse, AI-augmented workforce is fundamental to achieving collective goals and fostering innovation. Utilizing collaborative tools and platforms enhances this communication, especially in remote and hybrid work environments.

Emotional intelligence and empathy are equally crucial. By enhancing self-awareness, self-regulation, motivation, empathy, and social skills, individuals can navigate the complexities of modern work environments more effectively. These skills improve leadership, team dynamics, and workplace culture, contributing to higher levels of employee engagement and satisfaction. Strategies such as perspective-taking and active listening help in developing empathy, which is essential for conflict resolution and stress management.

Teamwork in an AI-augmented workplace requires a blend of human creativity and AI efficiency. Diverse teams bring together varied perspectives that drive innovation and inclusivity. Effective teamwork leverages AI to handle routine tasks, allowing human team members to focus on strategic and creative endeavors. Managing remote and hybrid teams through best practices and balancing individual and collective efforts ensures that all team members contribute meaningfully to project outcomes.

Conflict resolution and negotiation skills play a pivotal role in maintaining a harmonious work environment. Understanding the sources of conflict and employing techniques like mediation and collaborative problem-solving helps resolve disputes constructively. Negotiation skills are essential for reaching mutually beneficial agreements, ensuring that the interests of all parties are considered and addressed.

Balancing technical abilities with soft skills is essential to thrive in the modern workplace. While technical proficiency is necessary to operate and manage AI technologies, it is the soft skills that enable individuals and teams to apply these technologies effectively and ethically. A harmonious blend of these skills ensures that organizations can navigate technological advancements while fostering a supportive and innovative work culture.

Part III: Leadership and Organizational Strategies

Navigating the transformative landscape shaped by artificial intelligence, the role of leadership and strategic organizational practices becomes paramount. "Leadership and Organizational Strategies" delves into the essential elements required for guiding organizations through the complexities of AI integration and fostering a workforce capable of thriving in this new era. This section highlights the importance of visionary leadership, innovative thinking, and strategic planning in harnessing the full potential of AI while ensuring ethical and inclusive growth.

The transformation driven by AI demands a new breed of leaders who are not only technologically literate but also adept at steering their organizations through the intricate landscape of AI integration. Leadership roles in AI transformation extend beyond traditional management, requiring a deep understanding of AI technologies and their implications. Developing AI literacy and strategic thinking is crucial for leaders to make informed decisions that align with organizational goals and leverage AI for competitive advantage.

Effective leadership in this context also involves leading with empathy and ethical considerations, ensuring that AI implementation is responsible and benefits all stakeholders. Encouraging innovation and experimentation within the organization fosters a culture of continuous improvement and agility, essential for navigating the rapidly evolving AI landscape. Building cross-functional leadership teams that combine diverse expertise and perspectives further strengthens an organization's ability to adapt and innovate.

Creating a workforce that is prepared for the demands of the AI era involves strategic initiatives in talent acquisition and retention.

Attracting and retaining talent with the necessary skills and mindset is fundamental to maintaining a competitive edge. Promoting a culture of innovation and continuous learning within the organization ensures that employees are constantly updating their skills and knowledge. Employee development and reskilling initiatives are critical for enabling workers to adapt to new roles and responsibilities brought about by AI advancements. Aligning workforce strategy with AI advancements ensures that the organization's human resources are effectively integrated with technological developments, maximizing productivity and innovation. Measuring and assessing workforce readiness helps organizations identify gaps and opportunities for improvement, ensuring that they remain agile and responsive to changing market conditions.

The AI economy is ripe with opportunities for dynamic job creation and entrepreneurship. Identifying these opportunities requires a keen understanding of emerging trends and the ability to anticipate future demands. Supporting entrepreneurship and innovation within and outside the organization fosters a vibrant ecosystem where new ideas and ventures can flourish. Public-private partnerships play a crucial role in facilitating job creation and economic growth, combining resources and expertise from various sectors to drive innovation.

Policy implications for a dynamic job market must be considered, with regulations and incentives designed to support a thriving, inclusive economy. Encouraging intrapreneurship within organizations promotes a culture where employees are empowered to innovate and drive change from within, contributing to the overall dynamism and resilience of the organization.

When we conclude this exploration of employability in the AI era, it will be important to recap the key insights and recommendations discussed throughout the book. The future outlook on work and employability in the AI age is one of continuous evolution, requiring a proactive and adaptable approach from individuals, organizations, and policymakers. A call to action emphasizes the need for collective effort in embracing change and fostering a culture of continuous improvement. The final thoughts on the human-AI partnership highlight the potential for a harmonious and productive collaboration, where technology enhances human capabilities and drives progress.

Chapter 7: Cultivating AI-Savvy Leaders

In the age of artificial intelligence, effective leadership has become more critical than ever. As organizations navigate the complexities of AI integration, leaders play a pivotal role in guiding their teams and ensuring successful transformation. Cultivating AI-savvy leaders who can harness the potential of AI technologies and drive strategic initiatives is essential for maintaining a competitive edge in today's fast-paced business environment.

Leadership in AI transformation is about more than just understanding the technology; it involves a profound shift in how leaders think, strategize, and interact with both human and AI counterparts. The importance of leadership in this context cannot be overstated. Leaders must bridge the gap between technical experts and business strategists, ensuring that AI initiatives align with organizational goals and deliver tangible benefits. They must inspire and motivate their teams, fostering a culture of innovation and continuous learning that embraces technological advancements.

The role of leaders in a technology-driven landscape is evolving rapidly. Traditional leadership skills such as decision-making, communication, and empathy remain crucial, but they must be augmented with a deep understanding of AI and its implications. Leaders must be able to interpret complex data, make informed decisions based on AI insights, and navigate ethical considerations surrounding AI use. They need to be agile, ready to adapt to new tools and methodologies, and capable of guiding their organizations through the uncertainties of digital transformation.

Moreover, AI-savvy leaders are responsible for ensuring that their organizations remain competitive by leveraging AI to enhance productivity, drive innovation, and improve customer experiences. They must champion AI literacy within their teams, encouraging continuous education and upskilling to keep pace with technological advancements. By fostering a collaborative environment where human and AI capabilities are seamlessly integrated, these leaders can unlock the full potential of AI.

In this chapter, we will explore the critical components of cultivating AI-savvy leaders. We will discuss the key leadership roles in AI transformation, strategies for developing AI literacy and strategic thinking, the importance of leading with empathy and ethical considerations, and the need to encourage innovation and experimentation. Additionally, we will examine the value of building cross-functional leadership teams that bring together diverse skills and perspectives to drive AI initiatives forward.

As we delve into these topics, it will become clear that the journey to becoming an AI-savvy leader is both challenging and rewarding. By embracing this journey, leaders can position their organizations for long-term success in an increasingly AI-driven world.

As organizations embark on AI transformation, leadership roles must evolve to meet the unique challenges and opportunities that AI technologies present. Effective leadership in this context involves not only guiding the integration of AI but also rethinking traditional leadership responsibilities to maximize the benefits of AI and mitigate its risks. This section delves into the specific responsibilities of leaders in AI integration, highlights case studies of successful AI leadership across various industries and examines the impact of AI on traditional leadership roles and responsibilities.

Leadership in AI transformation involves a multifaceted set of responsibilities. First and foremost, leaders must develop a clear vision for how AI will be integrated into their organization. This includes identifying the strategic goals that AI can help achieve, such as improving efficiency, enhancing customer experiences, or driving innovation. Leaders must then communicate this vision effectively to their teams, ensuring that all members understand the purpose and benefits of AI initiatives.

Another critical responsibility is fostering a culture of continuous learning and innovation. Leaders must encourage their teams to embrace new technologies, provide opportunities for upskilling, and create an environment where experimentation and risk-taking are valued. This involves not only technical training but also promoting soft skills such as adaptability and problem-solving.

Leaders must also oversee the ethical implementation of AI. This includes establishing guidelines for data privacy, ensuring transparency in AI decision-making processes, and addressing potential biases in AI algorithms. By prioritizing ethical considerations, leaders can build trust in AI systems both within their organization and with external stakeholders.

Several industries offer compelling examples of successful AI leadership. In healthcare, leaders at IBM Watson have pioneered the use of AI to analyze medical data and assist in diagnostics. By integrating AI into clinical workflows, they have enhanced the ability of healthcare professionals to diagnose and treat diseases more accurately and efficiently. IBM's leadership in this area involves continuous engagement with medical practitioners, ongoing refinement of AI tools based on user feedback, and a strong emphasis on data privacy and ethical use.

In the automotive industry, Tesla's leadership in AI integration is noteworthy. Under Elon Musk's vision, Tesla has leveraged AI to develop advanced driver-assistance systems and autonomous driving capabilities. This success stems from a clear strategic vision, substantial investment in AI research and development, and a culture that embraces technological innovation. Tesla's leadership exemplifies how a bold vision and commitment to AI can revolutionize an industry.

The retail sector provides another example with Amazon's use of AI for personalized customer experiences and supply chain optimization. Jeff Bezos and his leadership team have driven AI adoption to enhance recommendation engines, automate warehouses, and optimize logistics. By prioritizing AI as a core component of their business strategy, Amazon has maintained a competitive edge in the market.

AI transformation reshapes traditional leadership roles in several ways. Decision-making processes, for instance, are increasingly data-driven. Leaders must become adept at interpreting AI-generated insights and incorporating them into strategic decisions. This shift requires leaders to be comfortable with data analytics and to work closely with data scientists and AI specialists.

Communication strategies also evolve as leaders need to explain complex AI concepts in an accessible manner to various stakeholders, from employees to investors. Clear, transparent communication about AI initiatives and their expected impact is crucial for gaining buy-in and managing expectations. Moreover, leaders must navigate the balance between human and AI capabilities. They need to understand the strengths and limitations of AI and ensure that human creativity, judgment, and emotional intelligence complement AI's analytical power. This balance is essential for maximizing productivity and innovation while maintaining a human-centered approach.

Ethical leadership becomes increasingly important in the context of AI. Leaders must address concerns about job displacement, data privacy, and algorithmic bias. By establishing robust ethical guidelines and fostering an inclusive dialogue about AI's impact, leaders can build trust and ensure responsible AI use.

Developing AI literacy and strategic thinking is essential for modern leaders navigating the complexities of a technology-driven world. AI literacy empowers leaders to understand the fundamentals of AI, its potential applications, and its implications for their organizations. It enables them to engage in informed discussions with AI experts, make data-driven decisions, and anticipate the challenges and opportunities presented by AI technologies.

To acquire and enhance AI knowledge, leaders can engage in various strategies, such as attending workshops, webinars, and conferences focused on AI trends and innovations. Online courses and certifications from reputable institutions offer structured learning paths, covering topics from basic AI concepts to advanced machine learning techniques. Collaborating with AI professionals and participating in AI-focused communities can also provide valuable insights and practical knowledge.

Integrating AI insights into strategic decision-making processes involves leveraging AI-generated data and analytics to inform business strategies. Leaders should cultivate a mindset that values data-driven decision-making, encouraging the use of AI tools to analyze market trends, customer behavior, and operational efficiencies. This integration not only enhances the accuracy and speed of decision-making but also fosters a culture of innovation and continuous improvement within the organization.

Continuous learning in AI is facilitated by utilizing various tools and resources designed to keep leaders updated with the latest developments. Online platforms, industry reports, academic journals, and AI news websites provide a wealth of information and insights. Engaging with AI experts through networking events, mentorship programs, and industry forums further enriches a leader's understanding and application of AI. By committing to ongoing education and staying abreast of technological advancements, leaders can ensure they remain at the forefront of AI innovation and effectively guide their organizations through the evolving landscape of artificial intelligence.

Leading with empathy and ethical considerations is crucial in the era of AI-driven transformation. Empathy in AI leadership signifies the ability to understand and share the feelings of others, which is essential for building trust, fostering collaboration, and ensuring that technological advancements serve the broader human good. Leaders who demonstrate empathy can effectively bridge the gap between technology and the people it impacts, creating a more inclusive and supportive work environment.

Addressing ethical challenges in AI implementation involves proactively identifying and mitigating potential risks such as bias, privacy concerns, and the unintended consequences of AI decisions. Leaders must ensure that AI systems are designed and deployed with fairness, transparency, and accountability in mind. This includes establishing clear ethical guidelines and standards, conducting regular audits of AI systems, and being transparent about how AI decisions are made and used within the organization.

Frameworks for ensuring responsible and ethical AI use provide a structured approach to integrating ethical considerations into AI projects. These frameworks typically include principles such as fairness, accountability, transparency, and human oversight. By adopting these frameworks, organizations can systematically address ethical issues and build trust with stakeholders. Leaders play a critical role in championing these frameworks and ensuring that ethical considerations are woven into the fabric of the organization's AI strategy.

Balancing technological advancements with human-centric leadership involves prioritizing the well-being and development of employees alongside the pursuit of technological innovation. Leaders must recognize that while AI can drive efficiency and innovation, it is the human elements of creativity, judgment, and emotional intelligence that ultimately guide and enrich these technologies. By maintaining a focus on human-centric leadership, leaders can ensure that technological advancements enhance rather than detract from the human experience. This balance helps in fostering a work environment where employees feel valued and supported, even as they adapt to new AI-driven processes and tools. This holistic approach not only promotes ethical AI use but also strengthens the overall organizational culture, driving sustainable success in the age of AI.

Encouraging innovation and experimentation is essential for organizations aiming to thrive in an AI-driven landscape. Fostering a culture of innovation within teams and organizations begins with leadership that values creativity and is willing to invest in new ideas. Leaders must create an environment where employees feel empowered to explore, experiment, and challenge the status quo. This involves promoting an open-minded approach, where questioning existing processes and suggesting improvements are encouraged and rewarded.

Strategies for promoting experimentation and risk-taking include providing resources and support for innovative projects, such as time, funding, and access to advanced tools and technologies. Encouraging a fail-fast mentality, where setbacks are seen as learning opportunities rather than failures, helps build resilience and encourages continuous improvement. Leaders should celebrate both successes and lessons learned from unsuccessful attempts, fostering a safe space for experimentation.

Examples of innovative AI applications driven by leadership demonstrate the transformative potential of combining visionary leadership with cutting-edge technology. For instance, AI-driven predictive maintenance in manufacturing has significantly reduced downtime and operational costs, thanks to leaders who championed the integration of AI into their maintenance processes. In healthcare, AI-powered diagnostic tools have improved patient outcomes by enabling early detection of diseases, guided by leaders who prioritized investment in AI research and development.

Overcoming barriers to innovation in AI projects often requires addressing organizational inertia and resistance to change. Leaders must communicate the long-term benefits of AI initiatives and involve stakeholders at all levels in the planning and implementation process. Providing training and development opportunities helps alleviate fears and build the necessary skills for AI adoption. Additionally, fostering cross-functional collaboration breaks down silos and encourages the sharing of knowledge and ideas, further driving innovation.

Creating a culture that values and nurtures innovation and experimentation requires a commitment from leadership to continually support and invest in new ideas. By promoting risk-taking, celebrating innovative efforts, and addressing barriers proactively, organizations can harness the full potential of AI technologies and drive sustainable growth and success.

Building cross-functional leadership teams is crucial for navigating the complexities of AI integration within organizations. The value of diverse skill sets in leadership teams cannot be overstated. A team composed of individuals with varied expertise brings multiple perspectives to problem-solving and decision-making. This diversity fosters creativity and innovation, as each member contributes unique insights and approaches. Technical leaders provide the necessary understanding of AI technologies, while non-technical leaders offer strategic, operational, and customer-centric viewpoints. This blend of skills ensures comprehensive planning and execution of AI initiatives.

Creating and managing cross-functional teams requires deliberate strategies to ensure cohesion and productivity. One effective approach is to define clear roles and responsibilities for each team member, ensuring that everyone understands their contributions and how they fit into the broader goals of the project. Regular communication and collaboration are essential. Leaders should establish regular meetings and checkpoints to discuss progress, address challenges, and realign objectives as needed. It's also important to foster an environment of mutual respect and trust, where team members feel valued and are encouraged to share their ideas and concerns openly.

Enhancing collaboration between technical and non-technical leaders is vital for the success of AI projects. This collaboration can be facilitated through joint training sessions and workshops that bridge knowledge gaps and build a common understanding of AI's potential and limitations. Encouraging open dialogue and active listening helps to break down barriers and ensures that technical insights are aligned with strategic business goals. Leaders should also leverage collaborative tools and platforms that enable seamless communication and project management, further enhancing teamwork.

Case studies of successful cross-functional leadership in AI initiatives highlight the importance of this approach. For example, a retail company successfully implemented an AI-driven inventory management system by forming a leadership team that included data scientists, supply chain managers, and sales executives. The diverse team worked together to identify pain points, develop solutions, and ensure the system met both technical requirements and business objectives. Another example is a healthcare organization that integrated AI into its patient care processes. The leadership team, comprising IT specialists, medical professionals, and administrative leaders, collaborated to develop and implement AI tools that improved diagnostic accuracy and operational efficiency while maintaining a focus on patient care and ethical considerations.

Cultivating AI-savvy leaders involves several key components essential for navigating the complexities of an AI-driven world. Leaders must develop a clear vision for AI integration, fostering a culture of continuous learning and innovation within their organizations. They need to ensure ethical considerations are prioritized, guiding the responsible use of AI technologies. Effective communication and strategic thinking are crucial, enabling leaders to interpret AI-generated insights and incorporate them into business strategies. Additionally, building cross-functional leadership teams that bring diverse skill sets and perspectives together enhances the overall capability to implement AI successfully.

The future of leadership in an AI-driven world will see a continued evolution where traditional leadership qualities are augmented by technological proficiency. Leaders will need to stay abreast of rapid technological advancements and continuously update their knowledge and skills. The ability to balance human-centric qualities such as empathy, ethical judgment, and emotional intelligence with a strong understanding of AI will become increasingly important. This balance ensures that while AI enhances operational efficiency and decision-making, the human elements of creativity, trust, and ethical considerations remain at the forefront.

Balancing technological proficiency with human-centric leadership qualities is essential for long-term success. While AI can drive remarkable efficiencies and innovations, it is the human touch that provides context, creativity, and ethical oversight. Leaders who can seamlessly integrate these elements will not only navigate the complexities of AI transformation effectively but will also foster a work environment where both technology and humanity thrive. This holistic approach to leadership will be crucial in shaping a future where AI and human capabilities complement each other, driving sustained growth and positive societal impact.

Chapter 8: Building an AI-Ready Workforce

In today's rapidly evolving business landscape, the need for an AI-ready workforce has become paramount. As artificial intelligence continues to revolutionize industries, organizations must ensure their workforce is equipped with the necessary skills and knowledge to harness the full potential of these technologies. The integration of AI into business operations promises significant benefits, including increased efficiency, enhanced decision-making, and innovative solutions to complex problems. However, realizing these benefits requires more than just adopting new technologies; it demands a strategic approach to workforce development.

An AI-ready workforce plays a crucial role in maximizing the potential of AI technologies. Employees who are proficient in AI can effectively collaborate with these systems, leveraging their capabilities to drive business objectives. This includes understanding how to operate AI tools, interpret AI-generated data, and implement AI-driven solutions in everyday tasks. Moreover, a skilled workforce can identify new opportunities for AI applications, fostering innovation and maintaining a competitive edge in the market.

To build an AI-ready workforce, organizations must invest in continuous learning and development programs that address the evolving demands of AI technologies. This involves not only technical training but also promoting soft skills such as critical thinking, adaptability, and problem-solving. By fostering a culture of continuous improvement and innovation, businesses can ensure their teams remain agile and capable of navigating the complexities of AI integration.

In this chapter, we will explore strategies for talent acquisition and retention, focusing on attracting individuals with the skills needed for an AI-driven future. We will discuss the importance of promoting a culture of innovation and continuous learning, which is essential for keeping pace with technological advancements. Additionally, we will examine effective employee development and reskilling initiatives that help bridge skill gaps and prepare the workforce for new AI-related roles. Aligning workforce strategy with AI advancements and measuring workforce readiness will also be key topics, providing a comprehensive framework for building an AI-ready workforce.

By prioritizing the development of an AI-ready workforce, organizations can unlock the transformative potential of AI technologies. This not only enhances operational efficiency but also drives innovation, positioning businesses for long-term success in the increasingly AI-centric business environment.

Strategies for talent acquisition and retention in an AI-ready workforce begin with identifying the key skills and competencies necessary for success. This includes not only technical abilities such as proficiency in machine learning algorithms, data analysis, and AI programming languages, but also critical soft skills like problem-solving, adaptability, and effective communication. Understanding these requirements allows organizations to target their recruitment efforts more precisely, seeking out candidates who possess a balanced mix of technical and interpersonal skills essential for thriving in an AI-driven environment.

Recruiting AI talent involves adopting best practices that attract highly skilled professionals. This includes creating compelling job descriptions that clearly outline the roles and expectations, highlighting opportunities for growth and innovation within the company. Leveraging modern recruitment tools and platforms can help reach a broader audience and identify potential candidates more efficiently. Establishing strong relationships with academic institutions and participating in AI-focused events and conferences also provides access to emerging talent. Additionally, showcasing a company's commitment to cutting-edge AI projects and a culture of innovation can attract top candidates who are passionate about making significant contributions in their field.

Retention strategies are crucial for keeping top AI professionals engaged and motivated. Providing continuous learning opportunities, such as access to advanced training programs, workshops, and certifications, helps employees stay updated with the latest developments in AI and enhances their skill sets. Creating a clear career progression path and offering competitive compensation packages are also vital. Moreover, fostering a collaborative and inclusive work environment where AI professionals feel valued and supported encourages long-term commitment. Regular feedback and recognition of achievements further contribute to job satisfaction and employee retention.

Being able to leverage diversity and inclusion is another powerful strategy for enhancing talent acquisition in the AI field. Diverse teams bring a range of perspectives and ideas, which can drive innovation and improve problem-solving capabilities. By actively seeking candidates from varied backgrounds and creating an inclusive culture that supports all employees, organizations can attract a wider pool of talent and foster a more dynamic and creative workplace. This not only enhances the organization's ability to develop comprehensive AI solutions but also positions it as an employer of choice for top AI professionals from diverse demographics.

Promoting a culture of innovation and continuous learning is essential for any organization aiming to thrive in an AI-driven world. Fostering an innovative mindset within the workforce begins with leadership that values creativity and encourages employees to think outside the box. This mindset is crucial as it drives the exploration of new ideas and approaches, leading to groundbreaking solutions and improvements in business processes. An innovative culture is characterized by openness to change, a willingness to embrace new technologies, and a proactive approach to identifying opportunities for improvement.

Encouraging continuous learning and curiosity involves providing employees with the tools and resources they need to expand their knowledge and skills. This can be achieved through regular training programs, access to online courses, and opportunities for professional development. Leaders should model curiosity by staying informed about industry trends and sharing their insights with the team. Additionally, promoting a growth mindset, where challenges are viewed as learning opportunities rather than obstacles, helps to cultivate an environment where continuous improvement is the norm.

Creating an environment that supports experimentation and risk-taking is vital for innovation. Organizations should establish frameworks that allow employees to test new ideas and approaches without fear of failure. This includes providing the necessary resources, such as time, funding, and technology, to experiment and iterate on projects. Recognizing and rewarding efforts, even if they do not result in immediate success, reinforces the value of risk-taking and encourages a culture where innovation can flourish. Open communication channels and collaborative spaces also play a significant role in facilitating the exchange of ideas and fostering a spirit of experimentation.

Examples of companies with successful cultures of innovation include Google, which famously allows employees to spend a portion of their time working on projects of their choosing, leading to the development of products like Gmail and Google News. Another example is 3M, known for its "15% rule," which encourages employees to dedicate a percentage of their work hours to innovative pursuits. These companies exemplify how fostering a culture of innovation and continuous learning can lead to significant advancements and a competitive edge in the market.

Employee development and reskilling initiatives are crucial for maintaining a competitive edge in an era defined by rapid technological advancements. The first step in this process is identifying skill gaps within the workforce. This involves conducting comprehensive assessments to understand the current capabilities of employees and pinpointing areas where new skills are needed to meet future demands. Once these gaps are identified, organizations can plan targeted development programs designed to bridge them effectively.

Implementing effective reskilling and upskilling programs requires a strategic approach. Reskilling focuses on teaching employees entirely new skills to transition into different roles, while upskilling enhances their current skill sets to improve performance in their existing positions. These programs should be tailored to the specific needs of the organization and its employees, ensuring relevance and practical application. A combination of theoretical learning and hands-on practice can help employees integrate new skills more effectively.

Leveraging online learning platforms and in-house training is essential for the success of these initiatives. Online platforms offer flexibility and access to a vast array of courses, enabling employees to learn at their own pace and convenience. In-house training, on the other hand, can be customized to address the unique challenges and objectives of the organization. This blend of learning opportunities ensures that employees receive both the general knowledge and specific insights needed to excel in their roles.

There are numerous success stories of organizations that have effectively reskilled their workforce. For example, AT&T launched an extensive reskilling program to address the digital transformation of their industry. By investing in employee education and offering a variety of learning paths, they managed to upskill their workforce to meet new technological demands, ultimately driving innovation and maintaining their competitive edge. Similarly, Amazon's "Career Choice" program provides employees with funding for courses in high-demand fields, enabling them to develop new skills that align with future career opportunities, both within and outside the company.

Aligning workforce strategy with AI advancements is essential for maximizing the benefits of artificial intelligence within an organization. Ensuring alignment between business goals and AI strategy begins with a clear understanding of how AI can support and enhance the company's objectives. This involves identifying the specific business challenges and opportunities that AI can address and developing a cohesive strategy that integrates AI initiatives with broader organizational goals. Leaders must communicate this vision effectively, ensuring that all team members understand how AI projects align with the company's mission and contribute to its success.

Developing a workforce strategy that complements AI initiatives requires a comprehensive approach to workforce planning and development. Organizations must assess their current capabilities and determine the skills needed to support AI-driven projects. This involves not only technical skills but also competencies in data analysis, project management, and change management. By identifying these requirements, companies can design targeted training and development programs to build an AI-ready workforce. Additionally, workforce strategy should include creating roles and responsibilities that facilitate collaboration between AI specialists and other departments, ensuring that AI tools are effectively integrated into everyday operations.

Integrating AI tools to enhance productivity and efficiency is a critical component of this alignment. AI can automate routine tasks, allowing employees to focus on more strategic and creative activities. By leveraging AI for data analysis, process optimization, and customer engagement, organizations can improve decision-making and operational efficiency. It is important to provide employees with the necessary training to use these tools effectively and to create a supportive environment that encourages experimentation and innovation. This integration not only boosts productivity but also helps employees see the tangible benefits of AI, fostering greater acceptance and enthusiasm for new technologies.

Case studies of successful alignment between workforce strategy and AI implementation provide valuable insights. For instance, IBM has effectively aligned its workforce strategy with AI advancements by investing in extensive training programs and creating new roles focused on AI development and implementation. This strategic approach has enabled IBM to leverage AI across various functions, from customer service to supply chain management, significantly enhancing productivity and innovation. Another example is General Electric (GE), which has integrated AI into its industrial operations to predict equipment failures and optimize maintenance schedules. By aligning its workforce strategy with AI initiatives, GE has improved operational efficiency and reduced downtime, demonstrated the powerful impact of AI when integrated with a well-aligned workforce strategy.

Measuring and assessing workforce readiness for AI integration involves a structured approach to ensure that employees possess the necessary skills and competencies to effectively leverage AI technologies. Key metrics for evaluating workforce readiness include assessing technical proficiency, such as the ability to use AI tools and understand machine learning concepts, as well as soft skills like adaptability, problem-solving, and collaborative abilities. Performance indicators might also include the number of employees trained in AI-related skills, the completion rate of AI-focused training programs, and the application of AI solutions in day-to-day operations.

To accurately assess skill levels and identify gaps, organizations can utilize various tools and frameworks. Skills assessments and competency matrices help map out the current capabilities of employees against the desired skill set required for AI initiatives. These tools can highlight areas where training and development are needed. Additionally, learning management systems (LMS) can track the progress of individual learning journeys, providing data on course completions, certifications earned, and knowledge gained. This comprehensive approach ensures that both technical and soft skills are evaluated and developed systematically.

Continuous assessment and feedback loops are critical to maintaining workforce readiness over time. Regular performance reviews, combined with real-time feedback, allow organizations to monitor the progress of their employees and make necessary adjustments to training programs. Incorporating AI-driven analytics can provide deeper insights into learning effectiveness and identify emerging skill gaps. By establishing a culture of continuous learning and improvement, organizations can ensure that their workforce remains agile and capable of adapting to new AI developments.

Examples of companies that have successfully measured and improved workforce readiness offer valuable insights. For instance, Accenture has implemented a robust system for assessing and enhancing the AI skills of its workforce. Through a combination of online courses, immersive training sessions, and certification programs, Accenture continuously monitors and upgrades the competencies of its employees. Similarly, Siemens has developed a comprehensive framework to assess and develop the digital skills of its workforce, incorporating regular evaluations and tailored training modules to keep pace with technological advancements. These companies demonstrate that with the right metrics, tools, and continuous feedback mechanisms, it is possible to build and maintain an AI-ready workforce.

Building an AI-ready workforce involves a multifaceted approach that integrates strategic planning, continuous learning, and a culture of innovation. Central to this strategy is identifying the key skills and competencies required for AI integration, which include both technical proficiency and essential soft skills. Organizations must adopt best practices for recruiting AI talent and implementing robust reskilling and upskilling programs to bridge skill gaps and enhance employee capabilities. Leveraging online learning platforms and in-house training ensures that employees have access to the latest knowledge and tools, fostering a culture of continuous improvement.

Ongoing development and alignment with AI advancements are crucial for maintaining workforce readiness. As AI technologies evolve, organizations must regularly assess their workforce's skills and competencies, using tools and frameworks to identify emerging gaps. Continuous assessment and feedback loops help monitor progress and adapt training programs, accordingly, ensuring that employees remain proficient in the latest AI technologies and methodologies. This proactive approach not only keeps the workforce agile but also aligns individual development with organizational goals.

Creating a sustainable and dynamic workforce capable of leveraging AI technologies for long-term success requires a commitment to fostering an innovative mindset. Encouraging experimentation, risk-taking, and a growth-oriented culture allows employees to explore new ideas and solutions without fear of failure. By celebrating both successes and learning experiences, organizations can cultivate an environment where creativity thrives. Additionally, building cross-functional leadership teams that integrate diverse skill sets enhances collaboration and drives AI initiatives forward.

Chapter 9: Dynamic Job Creation and Entrepreneurship

In an era defined by rapid technological advancements, artificial intelligence is reshaping industries and economies, profoundly impacting job creation and entrepreneurship. This transformative technology has the potential to create new opportunities, drive economic growth, and redefine the nature of work. As AI continues to evolve, it not only automates routine tasks but also opens the door to innovative business models, products, and services that were previously unimaginable.

The transformative impact of AI on job creation and entrepreneurship is multifaceted. On one hand, AI technologies can displace certain jobs, especially those involving repetitive tasks. On the other hand, they simultaneously generate new roles that require specialized skills in AI development, data analysis, and human-AI collaboration. This dual effect necessitates a proactive approach to workforce development and job creation, ensuring that workers are prepared for the emerging job landscape. Additionally, AI fosters entrepreneurial ventures by lowering the barriers to entry for new businesses, enabling startups to leverage advanced tools and data to compete with established companies.

The importance of dynamic strategies to harness opportunities in the AI-driven economy cannot be overstated. Traditional approaches to job creation and business development may not suffice in this rapidly changing environment. Instead, a dynamic and flexible strategy is required, one that embraces continuous learning, innovation, and adaptability. This involves fostering an entrepreneurial mindset, encouraging experimentation, and supporting new business ventures through public and private initiatives. Moreover, policies and partnerships that promote skill development and innovation are crucial for building a resilient economy capable of thriving amidst technological disruptions.

In this chapter, we will explore how AI is driving dynamic job creation and entrepreneurship. We will delve into strategies for identifying opportunities in the AI economy, supporting entrepreneurship and innovation, and the critical role of public-private partnerships in job creation. Additionally, we will examine the policy implications for a dynamic job market and discuss how encouraging intrapreneurship within organizations can further enhance growth and adaptability. Through these discussions, we aim to provide a comprehensive understanding of how to navigate and leverage the AI-driven economic landscape for sustained success and development.

Identifying opportunities in the AI economy begins with analyzing current and emerging trends. By staying informed about technological advancements and market shifts, businesses can pinpoint areas where AI is poised to make significant impacts. Trends such as machine learning, natural language processing, and automation are reshaping various sectors, offering clues about where the next wave of AI-driven innovation might occur. Understanding these trends helps businesses anticipate changes and position themselves strategically to capitalize on new opportunities.

Certain sectors and industries show particularly high potential for AI-driven job creation. Healthcare, for instance, is experiencing transformative changes through AI applications in diagnostics, treatment planning, and patient care management. AI is also revolutionizing the finance sector with predictive analytics, fraud detection, and personalized financial services. Manufacturing is benefiting from AI through enhanced automation, predictive maintenance, and supply chain optimization. Retail is leveraging AI for personalized customer experiences, inventory management, and sales forecasting. Identifying these high-potential areas allows businesses to focus their efforts where AI can offer the most substantial benefits.

Case studies of successful ventures and startups leveraging AI provide valuable insights into how these technologies can drive business growth and job creation. For example, companies like

Zebra Medical Vision have used AI to develop advanced diagnostic tools that improve patient outcomes and create new roles in AI development and healthcare analysis. Startups like UiPath have pioneered robotic process automation, significantly enhanced business efficiencies and creating a new market for automation specialists. These examples illustrate the diverse applications of AI and the economic opportunities they generate.

Tools and resources for identifying AI-related opportunities are essential for businesses looking to navigate the AI economy. Market research reports, industry conferences, and academic publications offer detailed analyses and forecasts about AI trends and developments. Online platforms like LinkedIn Learning and Coursera provide courses that keep professionals up-to-date with the latest AI technologies and their applications. Networking with industry experts, joining AI-focused professional groups, and participating in innovation hubs and incubators can also provide firsthand insights and collaborative opportunities.

We must learn to identify opportunities in the AI economy which involves a thorough analysis of current and emerging trends, focusing on sectors with high potential for AI-driven job creation, learning from successful ventures, and leveraging a variety of tools and resources. By adopting a proactive and informed approach, businesses can effectively position themselves to capitalize on the transformative potential of AI, driving innovation, growth, and job creation in the process.

Supporting entrepreneurship and innovation is crucial for driving economic growth and technological advancement in the AI era. Creating a robust entrepreneurial ecosystem begins with developing strategies that nurture and sustain startups and innovative projects. This involves fostering a culture that values creativity and risk-taking, where new ideas are encouraged and supported. Governments, educational institutions, and private sectors need to collaborate to provide a conducive environment for entrepreneurship.

Access to funding, mentorship, and resources is vital for AI startups to thrive. Securing financial support through venture capital, angel investors, and government grants can provide the necessary capital to turn innovative ideas into viable businesses. Additionally, offering mentorship programs that connect budding entrepreneurs with experienced business leaders and AI experts can provide invaluable guidance. Resources such as cutting-edge technology, office space, and research facilities also play a significant role in helping startups overcome initial barriers.

Building networks and communities that support AI entrepreneurs enhances collaboration and knowledge sharing. Creating platforms where entrepreneurs can connect, share experiences, and collaborate on projects fosters a sense of community and collective growth. Professional associations, online forums, and local meetups provide spaces for networking, learning, and forming strategic partnerships. These communities can drive innovation by pooling diverse skills and perspectives to solve complex problems.

Examples of innovation hubs and incubators highlight how structured support systems can drive AI entrepreneurship. Institutions like Silicon Valley's Y Combinator and MIT's The Engine provide comprehensive support to startups, including funding, mentorship, and access to a broad network of industry contacts. These hubs not only accelerate the growth of individual startups but also contribute to the overall ecosystem by creating success stories that inspire and attract further investment and talent.

The role of public-private partnerships in job creation is pivotal, particularly in the context of fostering AI innovation. Collaboration between government and industry is significant because it combines the strengths of both sectors: the regulatory and financial support of the public sector with the agility and innovation of the private sector. Such partnerships can drive job creation by facilitating the development of new technologies, creating an environment conducive to business growth, and ensuring that the workforce is equipped with the necessary skills.

Successful models of public-private partnerships in AI innovation showcase how these collaborations can lead to significant advancements. For instance, the European Union's Horizon 2020 program has funded numerous AI research projects by partnering with private companies, universities, and research institutions. This initiative has accelerated AI development and created high-tech jobs across the continent. Similarly, the U.S. government's partnership with tech giants through initiatives like the AI Next campaign aims to advance AI technologies while fostering job growth and innovation.

Case studies highlight the profound impact of public-private partnerships on local economies. For example, the partnership between the Singapore government and IBM has led to the establishment of the IBM Center for Blockchain Innovation. This center not only advances blockchain and AI technologies but also creates jobs and develops local expertise. Another case is the collaboration between the Canadian government and various AI startups through the Vector Institute in Toronto, which has positioned Canada as a leader in AI research and has significantly boosted the local economy by attracting talent and investment.

Strategies for developing and sustaining effective public-private initiatives involve clear communication, shared goals, and mutual benefits. Governments can provide incentives such as tax breaks, grants, and subsidies to encourage private sector participation. Establishing clear frameworks and regulations that support innovation while ensuring ethical standards and public trust is essential. Regular dialogues and consultations between public and private entities help align their objectives and adapt to changing circumstances. Additionally, continuous monitoring and evaluation of these partnerships ensure they meet their goals and provide opportunities for improvement.

Government policies play a crucial role in shaping the AI job market, determining how well economies can adapt to and benefit from technological advancements. Effective policies can drive AI-driven job creation by fostering an environment that encourages innovation, investment, and skill development. Governments must craft policies that not only facilitate the growth of AI industries but also ensure that the workforce is adequately prepared for the changes these technologies bring.

To support AI-driven job creation and workforce development, several policy recommendations can be made. First, investing in education and training programs that focus on AI and related fields is essential. This includes integrating AI literacy into school curricula and providing upskilling opportunities for the current workforce. Policies that encourage public-private partnerships in education can enhance the relevance and quality of training programs. Additionally, providing incentives for businesses to adopt AI technologies and create new roles can stimulate job growth.

Addressing the ethical and social implications of AI within policy frameworks is also paramount. Governments need to establish regulations that ensure AI technologies are developed and used responsibly. This includes setting standards for data privacy, preventing algorithmic bias, and ensuring transparency in AI decision-making processes. Policies should also promote equitable access to AI benefits, preventing the widening of socioeconomic gaps and ensuring that advancements in AI contribute to overall societal well-being.

Examples of successful policy interventions highlight the potential of well-crafted policies to stimulate job growth. In Finland, the government's AI strategy includes a focus on education and training, with initiatives such as the free Elements of AI online course, which aims to educate citizens about AI. This has helped create a more informed and skilled workforce, ready to engage with AI technologies. In South Korea, government initiatives have provided substantial funding for AI research and development, resulting in the creation of numerous startups and new job opportunities in the tech sector.

Encouraging intrapreneurship within organizations is crucial for fostering innovation and maintaining a competitive edge in a rapidly evolving market. Entrepreneurial thinking within established companies drives internal innovation, encourages risk-taking, and leverages employees' creative potential to develop new products, services, and processes. By cultivating an intrapreneurial culture, companies can harness the innovative spirit often found in startups while benefiting from the resources and stability of a larger organization.

Promoting intrapreneurship and innovation from within involves several key strategies. First, organizations must create an environment that encourages experimentation and tolerates failure. This can be achieved by providing employees with the freedom and resources to explore new ideas without the fear of negative consequences if they do not succeed. Additionally, establishing dedicated innovation teams or labs within the company can serve as incubators for new ideas, allowing intrapreneurs to focus on developing their concepts with minimal bureaucratic interference. Open communication and collaboration across departments also foster a culture where ideas can cross-pollinate and grow into innovative solutions.

Case studies of companies that have successfully implemented intrapreneurial initiatives provide valuable insights. For instance, Google's famous "20% time" policy allows employees to spend a portion of their work hours on projects outside their regular responsibilities. This policy has led to the creation of some of Google's most successful products, including Gmail and Google News. Another example is 3M, which has a long-standing tradition of encouraging employees to dedicate a percentage of their time to innovative projects. This approach has resulted in significant innovations, such as the invention of the Post-it Note.

Tools and frameworks for supporting and rewarding intrapreneurial efforts are essential for sustaining an intrapreneurial culture. These include providing access to innovation funds that employees can use to develop their projects, offering training and development programs focused on entrepreneurial skills, and implementing mentorship schemes that pair intrapreneurs with experienced leaders who can guide their efforts. Recognition and rewards are also critical; organizations should celebrate intrapreneurial successes through awards, promotions, and other incentives to demonstrate the value placed on innovation.

Dynamic job creation and entrepreneurship in the AI economy rely on a multifaceted approach that encompasses several key strategies. Identifying opportunities in the AI economy involves staying informed about current and emerging trends, focusing on high-potential sectors, learning from successful ventures, and leveraging a variety of tools and resources. Supporting entrepreneurship and innovation requires fostering a robust entrepreneurial ecosystem, ensuring access to funding, mentorship, and resources, building supportive networks and communities, and learning from successful innovation hubs and incubators.

Public-private partnerships play a crucial role in job creation by combining the strengths of government and industry, driving AI innovation, and implementing effective policy interventions. Policies must support AI-driven job creation and workforce development, address ethical and social implications, and learn from successful examples globally. Encouraging intrapreneurship within organizations involves fostering entrepreneurial thinking, promoting innovation from within, implementing supportive tools and frameworks, and recognizing and rewarding intrapreneurial efforts.

The importance of a collaborative approach involving entrepreneurs, governments, and organizations cannot be overstated. Collaboration ensures that resources are maximized, efforts are aligned, and the benefits of AI are widely distributed. Entrepreneurs bring innovative ideas and agility, governments provide regulatory frameworks and support, and organizations offer the infrastructure and market access needed for scaling. By working together, these stakeholders can create a robust ecosystem that fosters innovation, supports job creation, and drives economic growth.

Fostering a vibrant and adaptable job market capable of thriving in the age of AI requires continuous effort and commitment from all sectors. It involves embracing change, investing in education and skill development, and promoting a culture of innovation and adaptability. As AI continues to transform industries and redefine job roles, it is essential to ensure that the workforce is prepared for these changes. This preparation includes not only technical skills but also the soft skills needed to navigate a rapidly evolving landscape. By cultivating an environment that supports continuous learning and innovation, we can create a dynamic job market that not only adapts to the challenges of AI but also harnesses its potential to drive long-term success and prosperity.

Conclusion

Throughout this book, we have explored the profound impact of artificial intelligence on the job market and workforce. As AI technologies continue to evolve and integrate into various sectors, it is essential for individuals, organizations, and policymakers to adapt proactively to these changes. The AI-driven job market presents both challenges and opportunities, and navigating this landscape requires strategic foresight, continuous learning, and a commitment to innovation.

We began by examining the limitations of traditional education models and the necessity of reimagining education to include AI and technology integration. Developing critical thinking, creativity, and problem-solving skills has become crucial for future employability. Lifelong learning and continuous development emerged as central themes, highlighting the need for individuals to remain active learners throughout their careers. Strategies for self-directed learning, utilizing online resources, and balancing formal and informal learning opportunities were emphasized.

In discussing workforce adaptation, we underscored the importance of embracing flexible work arrangements and the rise of the gig economy. The significance of human-AI collaboration was explored, emphasizing the need for enhanced interpersonal and communication skills, emotional intelligence, and empathy. We delved into the evolving nature of teamwork, the impact of AI on job roles, and the essential skills required for thriving in an AI-augmented workplace.

Leadership and organizational strategies were also a focal point, with an emphasis on cultivating AI-savvy leaders who can navigate the AI transformation with strategic thinking and ethical considerations. Building an AI-ready workforce requires effective talent acquisition and retention strategies, promoting a culture of innovation, and aligning workforce strategies with AI advancements. We also explored dynamic job creation and entrepreneurship, highlighting the potential of AI to drive economic growth and the importance of supporting entrepreneurial ventures.

Key strategies for fostering employability and leveraging AI advancements were reiterated for individuals, organizations, and policymakers. For individuals, continuous learning and skill development are paramount. Embracing a growth mindset, actively seeking education and training opportunities, and staying informed about industry trends are critical steps to maintaining competitiveness. Organizations must invest in employee development, create supportive environments for innovation, and implement AI ethically and responsibly. Policymakers play a vital role in shaping the AI job market through supportive policies, public-private partnerships, and addressing the ethical and social implications of AI.

Education, continuous learning, and skill development are the cornerstones of adapting to the AI-driven job market. As technological advancements reshape industries, the ability to learn and adapt becomes a fundamental competency. This book has underscored the necessity of fostering a culture of lifelong learning and innovation, where individuals are equipped with the skills needed to thrive in an ever-changing environment.

By embracing these key insights and recommendations, we can create a workforce that is not only prepared for the challenges of the AI era but also poised to leverage its opportunities for growth and success. The journey ahead is one of continuous learning, adaptability, and collaboration, ensuring that both individuals and organizations can navigate the complexities of the AI-driven future with confidence and resilience.

The future outlook on work and employability in the AI age is characterized by rapid technological advancements and significant shifts in job roles and industries. As AI continues to dominate the landscape, several emerging trends and predictions provide a glimpse into the evolving nature of work. Automation of routine tasks will increase, allowing human workers to focus on more complex and creative endeavors. This shift will lead to the creation of new job roles that require advanced cognitive skills, emotional intelligence, and the ability to work alongside AI systems.

Potential new job roles and industries are expected to emerge as AI technologies evolve. Roles such as AI ethicists, who ensure ethical guidelines and practices are followed in AI development, will become increasingly important. Data scientists and machine learning engineers will continue to be in high demand, but new hybrid roles that combine technical expertise with domain-specific knowledge will also arise. For instance, healthcare AI specialists who understand both medical practices and AI technology will play a crucial role in integrating AI into patient care. Industries such as autonomous transportation, smart manufacturing, and personalized education will flourish, driven by innovations in AI.

Staying ahead of technological changes and preparing for future shifts in the job market is crucial for maintaining employability. Continuous learning and skill development are essential strategies for individuals to remain relevant and competitive. Embracing a mindset of lifelong learning and being proactive in acquiring new skills will be vital. This includes not only technical skills related to AI and data analysis but also soft skills such as adaptability, problem-solving, and effective communication. Organizations must foster a culture of continuous improvement, providing employees with opportunities for reskilling and upskilling to meet the demands of an AI-driven environment.

In addition to individual efforts, collaboration between educational institutions, businesses, and governments is necessary to create an ecosystem that supports the workforce in navigating these changes. Educational curricula must adapt to include AI literacy and technical training, while businesses should invest in ongoing employee development programs. Policymakers need to establish frameworks that promote innovation while addressing the social and ethical implications of AI.

The future of work in an AI-dominated landscape promises both challenges and opportunities. By staying informed about emerging trends, being open to new roles and industries, and committing to continuous learning, individuals and organizations can thrive in this dynamic environment. The key to success lies in the ability to anticipate and adapt to changes, leveraging AI technologies to enhance productivity, drive innovation, and create meaningful work experiences. As we move forward, the synergy between human ingenuity and AI capabilities will redefine the nature of work, shaping a future where both can coexist and complement each other.

The advent of AI demands a proactive response from individuals, organizations, and policymakers to harness its potential and mitigate its challenges. Individuals must take charge of their personal and professional growth by actively seeking opportunities for learning and skill enhancement. This includes engaging in continuous education through online courses, workshops, and certification programs that focus on AI and related fields. Staying curious and adaptable is crucial, as is developing both technical skills and soft skills like problem-solving and emotional intelligence. By doing so, individuals can remain competitive and prepared for the evolving job market.

Organizations have a significant role to play in preparing their workforce for the AI era. Investing in workforce development is essential, which means providing employees with access to training programs, learning resources, and opportunities for career advancement. Organizations should foster a culture of innovation, where creative ideas are encouraged, and employees are empowered to experiment and take risks. Supporting intrapreneurship within the company can drive internal innovation and help develop new products and services. Additionally, organizations must ensure that their use of AI is ethical and transparent, building trust with employees and customers alike.

Policymakers are tasked with creating a supportive framework that promotes job creation, ethical AI use, and effective public-private partnerships. This involves crafting policies that encourage investment in AI research and development, as well as in education and training programs that prepare the workforce for AI-driven changes. Policymakers should also address the ethical implications of AI, ensuring that regulations are in place to prevent biases, protect privacy, and maintain transparency in AI applications. Promoting collaboration between the public and private sectors can facilitate innovation and drive economic growth, ensuring that the benefits of AI are widely shared.

A coordinated effort from individuals, organizations, and policymakers is essential to navigate the complexities of the AI age. Individuals must embrace lifelong learning and skill development, organizations should invest in their workforce and foster a culture of innovation, and policymakers need to create an environment that supports ethical AI use and economic growth. By working together, we can build a future where AI drives progress and prosperity, benefiting society as a whole.

Embracing change and continuous improvement is fundamental to achieving long-term success in the rapidly evolving landscape of the AI-driven job market. A mindset that welcomes change and seeks continuous improvement is crucial for individuals and organizations alike. This approach fosters a culture of resilience and innovation, enabling both to thrive amid constant technological advancements and shifting market demands.

The need for flexibility and adaptability in navigating the evolving job landscape cannot be overstated. As AI and other technologies reshape industries, the ability to pivot and adjust to new circumstances becomes a key competitive advantage. Flexibility allows individuals to embrace new roles and opportunities, while adaptability ensures that organizations can swiftly respond to changes in the market. By being open to change and willing to learn, individuals and organizations can stay ahead of trends and capitalize on new opportunities.

Cultivating resilience and a growth mindset involves several practical strategies. First, it is essential to view challenges and setbacks as opportunities for learning and growth rather than as failures. This perspective helps build resilience and encourages a proactive approach to problem-solving. Engaging in continuous learning, whether through formal education, online courses, or self-directed study, keeps skills up-to-date and fosters intellectual curiosity. Setting realistic goals and celebrating small achievements along the way can also reinforce a growth mindset.

Building a supportive network is another important aspect. Surrounding oneself with mentors, peers, and colleagues who encourage and inspire can provide valuable insights and motivation. Regularly seeking feedback and being open to constructive criticism helps identify areas for improvement and facilitates personal and professional development. Additionally, practicing self-care and maintaining a healthy work-life balance ensures that individuals have the energy and mental clarity needed to tackle new challenges effectively.

Change and continuous improvement is vital for navigating the complexities of the AI-driven job market. By fostering a mindset that values flexibility, adaptability, and resilience, individuals and organizations can position themselves for long-term success. Practical steps such as continuous learning, setting realistic goals, building supportive networks, and maintaining a healthy balance are essential for cultivating a growth mindset and thriving in an ever-changing environment.

Final thoughts on the human-AI partnership underscore the profound potential that lies in the collaboration between humans and artificial intelligence. This partnership brings together the best of both worlds: the unmatched computational power and data processing capabilities of AI, and the creativity, empathy, and ethical judgment of humans. When these complementary strengths are effectively harnessed, they can drive unprecedented levels of innovation and efficiency. AI can handle vast amounts of data, perform repetitive tasks with precision, and provide insights that inform decision-making. Meanwhile, humans bring critical thinking, contextual understanding, and the ability to navigate complex social and ethical landscapes.

As we integrate AI into the workforce, it is crucial to address the ethical considerations and responsibilities that come with it. Ensuring that AI systems are designed and used ethically involves safeguarding data privacy, preventing algorithmic bias, and maintaining transparency in AI processes. Organizations and developers must prioritize these ethical standards to build trust and ensure that AI benefits are equitably distributed. There is also a responsibility to manage the social impacts of AI, such as job displacement and the need for reskilling workers. By addressing these challenges proactively, we can create a framework that supports ethical AI use and promotes social good.

Looking ahead, the future of work in a world where humans and AI collaborate holds immense promise. This partnership has the potential to create a more innovative, efficient, and inclusive workplace. AI can enhance human capabilities, allowing workers to focus on tasks that require emotional intelligence, creativity, and complex problem-solving. This synergy can lead to the development of new industries and job roles that we have yet to imagine, fostering economic growth and opportunities for all. As we move forward, it is essential to maintain a balance where technological advancements are aligned with human values and needs.

In this optimistic vision of the future, humans and AI work together seamlessly, each augmenting the other's strengths. This collaboration not only drives technological progress but also enriches the human experience, creating workplaces that are dynamic, inclusive, and forward-thinking. By embracing this partnership with a focus on ethical considerations and continuous improvement, we can build a future where technology enhances human potential and contributes to a thriving, equitable society.

www.ingramcontent.com/pod-product-compliance
Lightning Source LLC
Chambersburg PA
CBHW052322220526
45472CB00001B/228